LOMBARDY

THE ITALIAN LAKES

PHILIP'S TRAVEL GUIDES

LOMBARDY
THE ITALIAN LAKES

JOHN FLOWER

PHOTOGRAPHY BY CHARLIE WAITE

GEORGE
PHILIP

Acknowledgements

It would be remiss of me not to express my gratitude to a large number of people who have provided assistance of one sort or another, or who have introduced me to parts of Lombardy which otherwise would certainly have remained unknown. My thanks therefore to: the Italian Tourist Board in London; Pilgrim Airways; the Settore Commercio, Turismo, Sport e Tempo Libero in Milan; the Mediocredito Lombardo; many local tourist offices and in particular those at Cremona and Mantua; countless individuals, some anonymous, but especially Roberto Bruni, Natascia Faustini, Paula Ferro, Amanda Gronau, Luisa Quartermaine and Diego Zancani. A special debt, however, has to be reserved for my good friends in the Boselli families, and for Dino and Olivia de Pasquale, whose hospitality and kindness over the years have been immense and without whom the completion of this book would have been infinitely more difficult. Finally my thanks once again to Andrew Best and Lydia Greeves, to Jan Chambers for her word-processing skills and by no means least to my family for their continuing patience and affectionate support.

British Library Cataloguing in Publication Data
Flower, J. E. (John Ernest) *1938–*
Lombardy: the Italian lakes.—(Philip's travel guides)
1. Italy. Lombardy. Visitors' guides
I. Title
914.5204929

ISBN 0 540 012149

Text © John Flower 1990
Photographs © Charlie Waite 1990
Maps © George Philip 1990

First published by George Philip Limited,
59 Grosvenor Street, London W1X 9DA

Printed in Italy

Contents

*We are on a hill. To our right we have a superb view —
rocks, a fertile plain and two or three lakes; to our left is
another, quite different in all its details, but every bit as
magnificent. Beautiful, luxuriant and richly green,
Lombardy stretches away in front of us until the horizon
disappears in the mists of Venice some thirty
leagues away.*
Stendhal, ROME, NAPLES AND FLORENCE IN 1817

Half-title illustration Such displays of greenery soften stonework and provide cool shade in Bergamo.

Title-page illustration The simple beauty of the western entrance to Sant'Ambrogio, founded in the early ninth century and Milan's most celebrated church after the cathedral.

Opposite page La Parrocchiale at Montichiari stands proudly above the surrounding fields of corn.

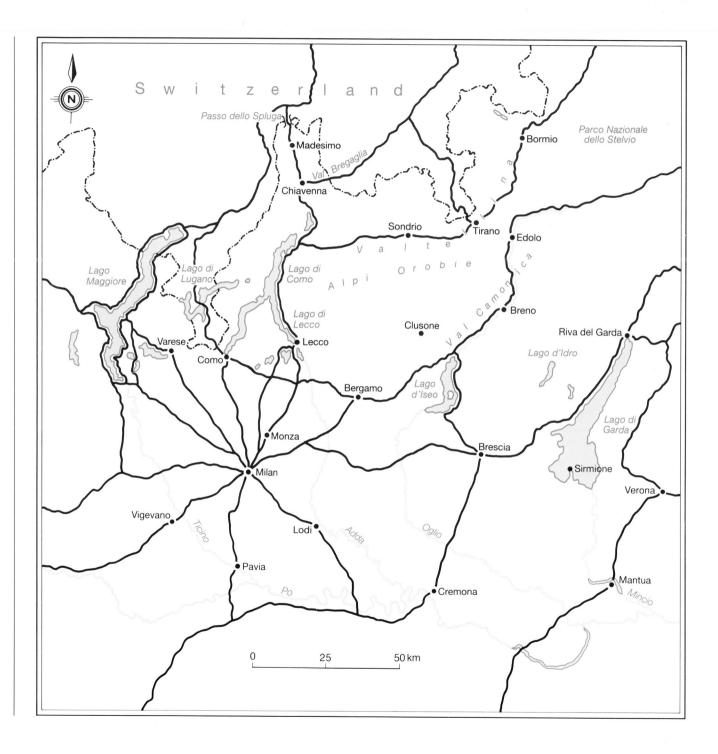

Introduction

Even though northern Italy was said to be 'replete with interest and instruction', intrepid travellers in the late nineteenth century might well have found that in other respects their trusty Baedeker guide was less than encouraging. Bandits, they were informed, were no worse than in any other European country, but trains were 'often behind time' and second-class hotels 'rarely very clean or comfortable'. If they were planning to take village accommodation, they were advised to sleep in 'iron bedsteads ... as they are less likely to harbour the enemies of repose', nor should they be surprised to find both pigs and poultry having free access to the houses in which they were staying. Substantially later, in 1930, advice is still strange to modern ears: 'Those who wish to take a small Medicine Chest with them, a proceeding strongly recommended to anyone making long independent excursions, should consult their physician at home as to the best drugs with which to stock it.'

Apart from the observation about trains, which may still all too often be valid, advice of this kind is, in general, a thing of the past. The modern traveller is encouraged to see Lombardy as a country of lakes and mountains, sailing and skiing, or to conjure up an image of Milan and its links with the worlds of business and fashion. This is hardly surprising.

Tourism is important. Italy's Great Lakes are the most famous, most attractive and amongst the biggest in Western Europe, with a combined area of about 1000 square kilometres; and while the Italian Alps may not rival those of Switzerland, or even France, they are impressive. With each year, too, Milan becomes an increasingly important national and international commercial centre.

Lombardy is the fourth largest of Italy's twenty regions and is one of the most varied scenically. The alpine fringe to the north, known as the Valtellina, is spectacular country, with several peaks rising to well over 3500 metres and large areas accessible only on foot. The principal lakes, like long, watery fingers, lie just to the south, their shores bordered by a lower but still dramatic country of wooded hills and valleys, with panoramic views of the mountains to the north. Further south still is the valley of the Po, flat and fertile and dotted with historic towns and villages. For much of its length the Po itself forms Lombardy's border with Emilia-Romagna, but just south of Pavia a small but delightful corner pushes further south into the foothills of the Apennines. Slightly west of centre and with a population fast approaching one quarter of the region's total of 9 million is Milan, the capital not only of Lombardy but of northern Italy as a whole.

The history of Lombardy is complicated and frequently punctuated with violence. There is evidence of prehistoric man, who left primitive rock carvings in the Val Camonica just north of Lake Iseo. The Etruscans, Umbrians and Celts all enjoyed periods of domination, but the region was given some stability for the first time under Roman rule when Milan, or Mediolanum, 'the middle city', developed as the capital. As the Roman Empire collapsed, northern Italy was attacked and plundered by Germanic tribes, the most important of which were the Langobardi or Lombards, who gave their name to the province. (It is also claimed by many Italians that the *milanesi* owe their above average height to these distant Germanic barbarians.) For a while the Holy Roman Emperor Charlemagne was overlord of the region and the capital shifted to Pavia, where he was crowned in 774. After the contraction of his empire and through the early Middle Ages, northern Italy was subject to almost continuous internal feuding and Lombardy was frequently caught up in the struggle between the Holy Roman Emperor and the Pope for dominance in Europe.

This period came to an end in the twelfth century, when local lords united in the Lombard League and succeeded in freeing themselves from the attentions of the Holy Roman Emperor by defeating the powerful and greedy Frederick Barbarossa at Legnano in 1176, only fourteen years after he had brought Milan to its knees. During the next four centuries the struggles were internal, with three families in particular emerging to found powerful dynasties: the Viscontis and Sforzas, whose dominion lay over Milan and the surrounding northern area, and the Gonzagas from Mantua to the east. All three have left their mark in a series of castles and palaces, symbols not only of military strength but also of statesmanship, accumulated wealth and patronage of the arts.

The Viscontis first made their claims through

The Ortles mountains overlook summer pastures at San Carlo west of Bormio.

Ottone, who became archbishop of Milan in 1262. A prelate of considerable political ambitions, he forged links with the Holy Roman Empire and succeeded in establishing power over a territory which stretched as far as Bologna, Genoa and Pavia. The most influential Visconti, however, was Gian Galeazzo (1351–1402), who became lord of Milan and master of the northern half of Italy, where he managed to achieve some kind of federal unification. He is remembered as an ambitious, ruthless man, but as one who also loved the arts and architectural splendour – he was responsible for founding the great Carthusian monastery at Certosa, just outside Pavia. Gian Galeazzo was succeeded by his son, Filippo Maria (1392–1447), but when he died without a male heir, the succession passed through an illegitimate line to Francesco Sforza (1401–66), who had previously fought for both Milan and its rival Venice in the struggle for power over northern Italy. It was Francesco who began the development of the canal system around Milan and expanded the region's agricultural activities. Finally, in 1480, Lodovico (1451–1508) – known as *Il Moro* on account of his colouring – became ruler of Milan. An enlightened, intelligent man who was a friend of Leonardo da Vinci and a great patron of the arts, Lodovico marks the high point of the Visconti-Sforza line.

About 120 kilometres to the east the Gonzaga family had emerged as an influential power in Mantua by the twelfth century. In 1328, having defeated the forces of the Bonacolsi family who had been ruling Mantua for the previous sixty years, Luigi Gonzaga (1568–91) was named Vicar General of Mantua and the family continued to rule virtually unchallenged until the early eighteenth century. Like the Viscontis, the Gonzagas produced great patrons. Isabella, for example, wife of Francesco II of Mantua, contributed enormously to the artistic wealth of the Palazzo Ducale in the early sixteenth century, while Vespasiano was responsible for designing Sabbioneta, one of Lombardy's most enchanting villages, in the sixteenth century.

Partly as a result of the relative political stability,

tracks provide access for some form of motorized transport. But essentially you have the impression that the basic pattern of life has remained unchanged for generations. This powerful sense of the past pervades the historic centres of cities and towns as well. *Palazzi* – town houses rather than palaces – from the seventeenth and eighteenth centuries are marvels of classical architecture; earlier examples reflect the wealth generated by medieval merchants. And around almost every corner you will see the façade of a church, with a soaring campanile alongside. Many of these buildings have been restored over the last hundred years or so, a process which has brought out the subtle shades of pink and pale orange that are so characteristic of their brickwork. Few sights are more beautiful than the flank of a church or a typical Lombardy tower, caught and warmed by the sunlight of a late summer evening.

Just as characteristic are the vast plains of the Ticino and Po valleys, cultivated with rice, maize and vegetables, and where frogs are reared in their thousands. In spring and early summer the plains are like great green oceans, but in winter, when the ground is snow covered, they can be bitterly cold and raw, or under torrential spring rain quickly transformed into a morass of tangled stalks and mud. The lakes, known for a microclimate in which exotic trees and flowers flourish and frequently described as resembling the Mediterranean, are quite magnificent on fine, sunny days. But they, too, have moods. In summer their atmosphere can become unbearably humid and in spring and autumn their surface whipped into a frenzy by sudden storms. High mountain valleys and passes surrounded by the most spectacular of vistas may seem almost artificially beautiful in fine weather, but become altogether different in snow, or thunderstorms. Streams and rivers which virtually disappear in the summer months can develop into raging torrents as the winter snows melt. In the Po valley and the southern reaches

---

This *cascina* in the Po valley is much restored and was once considerably more extensive.

of Lombardy they are carefully controlled and form part of an elaborate irrigation system, but elsewhere their force is a potential danger, as the Adda disaster in the Valtellina in July 1987 only too frighteningly demonstrated.

All this and more contributes to the real Lombardy. As in other regions of Italy, you can only marvel at the variety and richness to be sampled. But as elsewhere it is essential to get behind what is presented to the average visitor. The Shrove Tuesday celebration known as *Carnevale* is spectacular in Como, but it is often more charming, even if muted, in a tiny community elsewhere. Chance conversations in cafés, providing you can overcome a natural suspicion of foreigners in some of the more remote areas, are likely to be more revealing than many an official guide.

Where food is concerned, Lombardy is less easy to characterize, as there is no single dish which typifies the region as a whole. As elsewhere in Italy, you will find a wide range of cooked meats and cheeses, many of which are locally produced. Hams cured in the Valchiavenna or around Mantua have distinctive flavours of their own which local people instantly recognize; parmesan cheese, found in great rocks, is priced according to its vintage and has a sweetness undetectable in its supermarket cousin abroad. Pizza is found everywhere, but those from wood-fired ovens (*forno al legno*) have a special taste and Lombardy also offers the *calzone*, a pizza sandwich folded over its filling (this is worth sampling if only for its name – *calzone* means both 'purse' and 'trousers'!). There are also local specialities which should not be missed – *pizzocheria* (pasta cooked in butter and served with vegetables) from the Valtellina, *zuppa di pavese* (a raw egg on toast in hot soup) from Pavia, *stracotto di asino* (donkey stew) or *tortelli di zucca* (pasta cases filled with pumpkin and cooked in butter) from Mantua are only a few. And for those with a sweet tooth, there is the famous Milanese *panettone*, a cake stuffed with fruit and peel, or the *torrone*, a chewy mixture of almonds and honey. Nor should Lombardy wines be neglected, even though local people frequently display a surprising ignorance about them. From the Valtellina around

Sondrio come Grumello, Sassella and Inferno, sturdy, dry reds made from the Nebbiolo grape; south of Pavia, a pleasant dry white wine, Oltrepo Pavese, is produced and from the Franciacorta region near Brescia comes a sparkling white which can be treacherously refreshing on a hot day in August. Even though the methyl alcohol scandal in 1986 did untold damage to the Italian wine trade as a whole, the new classification DOCG (*Denominazione di Origine Controllata Garantita*), which has replaced the older DOC, normally guarantees a safe choice.

Finally, anyone setting out to explore Lombardy should know something of what they will find in the way of roads. Motorways (*autostrade*) radiating from Milan ensure rapid connections with most of the major towns, and the state roads are generally reliable, even though around Milan they are frequently congested. Secondary and minor routes vary enormously; some are well maintained, but others have poor surfaces and can be dangerous in winter conditions. Many turn into a series of tight hairpin bends as they snake up the side of a mountain, and the simple warning *tornante* is often insufficient for the way in which the road can cut back above you. This alone can be disconcerting enough,

---

Rezzonico on Lake Como enjoying the evening sun in autumn with boats already being put away for the winter.

but it is even more so when the blast of a horn announces the imminent arrival of a bus or lorry which you cannot yet see. But the reward for tackling these roads is that many of them take you to valleys and plateaux which cannot even be glimpsed from below. Tiny villages or farmsteads lie in wait, most of them giving the impression that they have barely changed over the centuries. In these mountain regions, particularly on the border with Switzerland and in the Stelvio park and Orobie Alps, there are many marked trails, some taking a week or more to complete, with overnight stops at a *rifugio*, a hostel where accommodation can vary from the most basic to the luxurious. Several *rifugi* are more than a hundred years old. Detailed maps for these walks can be purchased from local tourist offices, where you can also make arrangements to join a guided party.

I have organized this book around Milan, 'the middle city', as its Latin name demands. Each of the areas considered thereafter is self-contained, each has its own particular character. With the exception of the major lakes, Lombardy is far less well known than it deserves to be, though, like so much of Italy, it is extraordinarily rich in natural and artistic beauty. While there are some features which I have had to leave out and others I have inevitably missed, I hope I have provided sufficient foretaste of this beauty to encourage others to explore Lombardy and discover its delights for themselves.

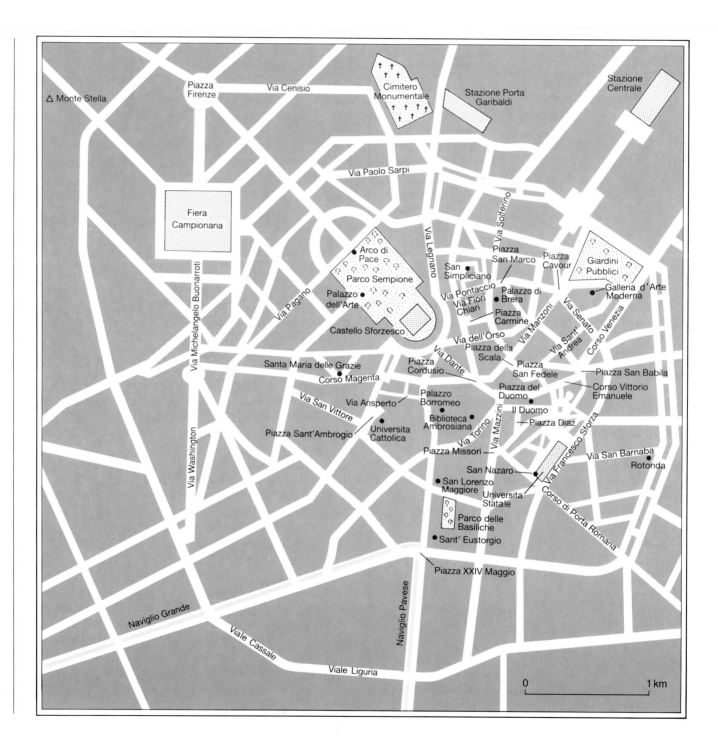

△ Monte Stella

Piazza Firenze

Via Cenisio

Cimitero Monumentale

Stazione Porta Garibaldi

Stazione Centrale

Via Paolo Sarpi

Fiera Campionaria

Via Solferino

Via Legnano

Arco di Pace

Piazza San Marco

Piazza Cavour

Giardini Pubblici

San Simpliciano

Parco Sempione

Via Pontaccio

Palazzo di Brera

Galleria d'Arte Moderna

Via Pagano

Palazzo dell'Arte

Via Fiori Chiari

Piazza Carmine

Via Manzoni

Via Senato

Corso Venezia

Castello Sforzesco

Via dell'Orso

Piazza della Scala

Via Sant' Andrea

Via Dante

Santa Maria delle Grazie

Via Michelangelo Buonarroti

Piazza Cordusio

Piazza San Fedele

Piazza San Babila

Corso Magenta

Piazza del Duomo

Corso Vittorio Emanuele

Via San Vittore

Via Ansperto

Palazzo Borromeo

Il Duomo

Piazza Sant'Ambrogio

Biblioteca Ambrosiana

Universita Cattolica

Piazza Diaz

Via Mazzini

Via Torino

Piazza Missori

Via Washington

San Nazaro

Via Francesco Sforza

Via San Barnaba

Rotonda

San Lorenzo Maggiore

Universita Statale

Corso di Porta Romana

Parco delle Basiliche

Sant' Eustorgio

Piazza XXIV Maggio

Naviglio Grande

Naviglio Pavese

Viale Cassale

Viale Liguria

0   1 km

1
The Middle City

The spirit of Milan in the late twentieth century is perfectly captured by two of the large pieces of modern sculpture scattered around the city. The first, just outside Linate airport to the east and carved from imitation white marble, resembles a massive interlocking Chinese puzzle. The second is in Piazza Diaz in the city centre just to the south of the cathedral. Here, on a grass mound in the centre of the square, is a giant polished caster. Curving up and over it are three sets of fins or wings splayed as though caught in a high wind. If the first is solid, challenging and aggressive, the second is balanced and full of potential energy and movement. Every one of these qualities is strikingly characteristic of one of Europe's most fascinating and exciting cities.

For the *milanesi*, there is no doubt that Milan is their nation's real capital. Rome may hold that position officially and is clearly supreme historically and in many ways culturally. But Milan is where things happen. The extraordinary amount of restoration work funded either by local government or by private institutions in the mid 1980s alone testifies to a thriving, proud and above all wealthy community.

The drive and energy for all this activity are much in evidence at Milan's international trade fairs, the best in the country and even, some would say, in Europe.

The permanent site for these, the Fiera Campionaria, welcomes over a million visitors during ten days in April, when more than a quarter of the country's annual trading deals are negotiated. Most of the money generated at these massive commercial events – and by tourism – passes through Milan's banks, for long the most important in Italy. It is worth visiting several of these in the commercial nerve-centre around Piazza Cordusio west of the cathedral. Not only do they offer the opportunity to sense Milan's prosperity and to marvel at the high level of technical expertise (until you are in a hurry to catch a plane and a computer breaks down), but they also display some of the grandest interior design in the city. Modernization has, of course, taken its toll. Plastic and glass may be much in evidence, but the grandiose scale of these buildings is still to be appreciated in the high, richly plastered ceilings and heavy wooden doors.

In the late eighteenth century an English lady, Mrs Piozzi, who had married an Italian music teacher, wrote from Milan that 'fashions do not change here as often as at London or Paris.' Times have changed, and more recently Milan has come to be recognized as one of the world's principal design and fashion centres, with elegant and expensive shops which rival any in Paris, London or Berlin. Affluence and style are characteristic of the successful middle classes, with their chic apartments filled with leather furniture and imaginatively designed lamps. The boldness and cut of their clothes is equally striking. And where else in the world is black worn by women of all ages with such elegance and panache? Women's sense of fashion generally is an expression of a sexual emancipation and confidence that has come with the growth of commercial prosperity.

Like most places that have experienced a boom of this dimension, Milan has been obliged to spread and has done so in all directions, especially to the north. An increase in rents – often fourfold in a few years – has pushed people away from the city centre. This movement, coupled with the influx from elsewhere, has created difficulties. In some cases villages which fifty years ago enjoyed their independence and some individual character have been absorbed by suburban sprawl. Arese to the north-west is a typical example. Twenty years ago the population was about three thousand; by the mid 1990s it will have nearly trebled. This growth rate in itself is not particularly dramatic, but local people are incensed at the way in which every newly available piece of 'green land' is being picked off by real estate developers and sacrificed to high-density, high-rise building.

An attempt to accommodate the already rapidly expanding population of Milan was begun in the 1960s with a programme of residential developments between 10 and 15 kilometres from the city centre. The new suburbs are prosaically known as Milano 2, Milano 3, Milago and Milanfiori. Some estates were state-financed; others private. A number have been successful, but signs of wear and tear and inadequate funding are all too often apparent. The districts of Gallaratese or Gratosoglio, for example, are distinctly shabby – an unappetizing mix of stark, uniform, high-rise apartment blocks, ugly pylons, patches of uncared-for grass, and cracked concrete and asphalt serving as football and basketball pitches. Litter and graffiti are plentiful. By contrast, the Milano 2 complex at Segrato to the north-west, developed with funding from private investment, is much more elegant. Build-ings are varied, more imaginatively designed and interestingly and attractively decorated. Many of the apartments have luxuriant balcony gardens, fast-growing trees have been planted in the grounds, and wisteria and ivy cover potentially unattractive concrete façades.

Yet whatever their individual qualities, such developments also contribute hugely to another consequence of this urban explosion – pollution. Although steps are being taken to combat it, the evidence is all too clear. The dullness of the water in the city's canals is a permanent and unpleasant reminder of a problem for which there appears to be no easy solution. Within hours of dawn, the sky above Milan invariably loses its brightness, as can be observed by anyone who climbs the 170-metre Monte Stella early in the morning. (This artificial hill, the most famous local landmark in Milan's inner suburbs, was built from rubble in the north-west area of the city during the post-war period of reconstruction.) In the Po valley, only fifty kilometres or so to the east, the mist which hangs over the river like a shroud has somewhat incongruously become a tourist attraction, despite the fact that pollution is largely responsible for it. Perhaps Milan's haze will also be seen as appealing.

Like Paris, the old centre of Milan resembles a spider's web. Medieval maps show it to be completely surrounded by walls and a waterway, and modern aerial photographs clearly reveal how new rings of development were added over the years. At the very centre is the cathedral – *il duomo* – with its piazza and nearby *galleria* (arcades), a natural focal point for *milanesi* and tourists alike. The nucleus of the city can be explored relatively easily on foot, certainly as far out as the line of the medieval canal to the south (now Viali Cassala and Liguria) or the superb cemetery, the Cimitero Monumentale, to the north. Not so very long ago cars parked on the pavements made walking both hazardous and unpleasant. More recently, the city authorities have installed steel hoops along the kerbs to keep the traffic in its place. Problem areas still remain, but in general it is now relatively easy to move around Milan on foot. But in indifferent weather, or for the less energetic, an excellent way of seeing the city is by the ubiquitous, if rather uncomfortable, orange trams. For a little over 2500 lire, a *tesserino turistico giornaliero* allows unlimited use of both tram and underground for a day. An ordinary ticket costing only 1000 lire purchases 75 minutes' travel on tram or bus. The network of routes is so complex and efficient that by hopping from one vehicle to another you can explore as wide an area as you wish; also, since trams have priority, it is possible to move across the city with relative ease. Trams are also good value for sampling the atmosphere in central Milan at different seasons or times of the day. Here you will see groups of chattering schoolchildren in the early morning, serious businessmen in the evening, families laden with presents at Christmas or Easter, exuberant (or downcast) football supporters returning on a Sunday from the San Siro stadium, home of Inter-Milan.

But it is by walking that the real discoveries are made. These will include the *salumeria*, where a selection from an unbelievable array of spiced meats, hams and pickled delicacies can be bought and sampled in small quantities; bakeries selling bread of every possible shape and variety; cheese shops with great rocks of parmesan or the softer *mozzarella*, *scaramozza* and *provolone* hanging from the ceiling like bunches of huge anaemic grapes; and fruit and vegetable stores where the produce is beautifully displayed, each item looking as though it has been individually polished. The Milan delicatessen Peck, where the assistants dress in white shirts with black bow-ties, is an international name. Its displays are dazzling; but so are the prices.

From any one of these establishments it is easy to buy food for a picnic which, weather permitting, you can eat in various agreeable locations, perhaps in the public gardens off Piazza Cavour or behind Castello Sforzesco, or in the square by the national university, Largo Richini. And should eating *al fresco* be neither appealing nor possible, Milan offers a wide range of alternatives, from the most basic and cheapest *pizzeria* (of which there are reputed to be over five hundred) to very expensive and often pretentious establishments.

The latter can present a problem. With little local traditional cuisine of its own, Milan's top restaurants, with two notable exceptions, tend to offer anonymous, international menus. These exceptions are the Osteria di Porta Cicca in Rippa Ticinese to the south; and the Bagutta in the street of the same name some 500 metres north-east of the cathedral, in the heart of the artists' and writers' *quartiero*. The walls here are covered with cartoons, caricatures, theatre notices and programmes; the clientele is very mixed and the service friendly. And, as in many restaurants, if you take the house wine you can drink – and pay for – as much as you like from the bottle left on your table.

In addition there are countless small bars and cafés differing widely in quality, atmosphere and price. In winter no visit to Milan is complete without sampling hot chocolate or real Italian coffee. The former is often so thick as to be almost gelatinous and is taken by a spoon as easily as it is drunk; the latter, even when commercially produced, is very strong and has an almost immediate revitalizing effect on flagging limbs. Laced with alcohol (*caffe corretto*), it is even more effective. Strolling around the commercial areas early in the morning before the day's work has begun in earnest is an invigorating experience, so sharp is the smell of freshly-ground coffee. That so many Italians should express their concern about its 'harmful' effect is scarcely believable!

Exploring central Milan on foot is best done in autumn or spring before the weather becomes either bitingly cold or stiflingly humid and hot. Four suggested tours, based on those in the Touring Club Italiano guide to northern Italy, start from Piazza del Duomo and go off in the direction of the four major segments of the compass. The Touring Club guide recommends using a car for parts of each, but in view of the cheapness and availability of public transport this is neither necessary nor even desirable.

The piazza itself is hemmed in rather incongruously between the ornate west façade of the cathedral and a bank of fluorescent-strip advertising above the stretch of road linking Via Mazzini and Via Mengoni. Much has inevitably been written about the cathedral. It was dismissed by D. H. Lawrence as 'an elaborate wedding-cake', but others have been more complimentary. The nineteenth-century French writer Stendhal, for example, whose *Voyages en Italie* contains a wealth of observations and anecdotes, described it as a 'forest of marble needles' and the English poet Shelley thought it 'a most astonishing work of art'.

Work on the cathedral began in 1386, but progress was very slow and the building was not completed until the nineteenth century. So many designers and craftsmen of various nationalities were employed during that long period that it is extraordinary the building should have the uniformity it does. In the twentieth century much restoration work has been carried out, first in the 1930s and again after the air-raids of 1943. From whatever angle it is approached, the cathedral dominates and dwarfs everything around it. It is topped by a great spire (one of 135) that was erected between 1765–9 and carries a gilded statue of the Virgin Mary. Set over 100 metres above the ground and illuminated at night, this forms a beacon for all Milan. From the foot of the spire and the roof – reached by lift or stairs from the south transept – there are superb views of the entire city and, on fine days, north to the Spluga pass into Switzerland and the Alps, west to Turin and south over Pavia and the Certosa.

The cathedral is best approached from the south along the narrow street separating the Museo di Duomo, containing its treasures and a collection of related manuscripts and books, and the episcopal palace. From here the apse can be seen in all its intricate detail, decorated with thin, fluted columns, gargoyles and over two thousand statues, a foretaste of the edifice as a whole. From a distance the outside of the building appears white (one reason, no doubt, for Lawrence's description), but on closer inspection the colour of the marble is seen to be wonderfully subtle, a mix of very pale shades of pink, grey, peach and fawn. The whole surface gives the impression of having been washed delicately with water-colours. Such subtlety is offset, however, by violence. If the gargoyles are of mixed design – some just gaping mouths, others monstrous in their ugliness – many of the statues are extraordinary. Some are of pensive, peaceful, humble folk making gestures of blessing; others depict figures fighting with their fellow-men or apocalyptic monsters, tortured or martyred. Many are suffering the terrible agony of some form of crucifixion. One, roped upside down to a tree, is desperately attempting to take the full weight of his body on his one free arm. . . . These are not only reminders of the punishments for a sinful existence here on earth, but stark illustrations of the dark side of so much of gothic art.

Inside the west door – one of five richly carved baroque doorways on this façade which are opened on feast days and special occasions – the cathedral is no less monumental. The central nave is flanked on each side by pointed arches supported on 26 massive compound pillars, their capitals fashioned as tabernacles. Above, supported on lighter vaulting, the roof continues to a height of over 65 metres. Once, just before Christmas when the cathedral was full of families, I saw a small child lose hold of his purple balloon and watched it float away into the vaults of the roof – a symbolic spirit, but also a reminder of just how huge the place is.

Despite being the second biggest church in Italy after St Peter's in Rome, the cathedral always seems busy, and not simply because of the tourists. Early morning mass is well attended as are the confessionals, and on major Christian feast days it is packed. Few services can be more moving than the Good Friday commemoration of Christ's crucifixion, the descent from the Cross and the laying of the body in the tomb. Throughout the year the cathedral is decorated according to the religious season. At Christmas, for example, the nave is hung with tapestries depicting scenes from the lives of the saints, and if you are lucky you will see a glass case containing the embalmed and red-robed body of the much-loved Cardinal Andrea Ferrari, who was Archbishop of Milan from 1894 until his death in 1921.

Christian martyrdom: two of the figures decorating the south side of Milan cathedral.

Milan cathedral: adoration of the Infant Jesus, detail from the west door (*left*); representatives of wisdom and authority from the south façade (*above*).

The finding of the infant Moses among the rushes. One of the Old Testament stories illustrated on the south side of Milan cathedral.

Much of the carving and ornamentation is heavy, such as the splendidly baroque canopied chapel dedicated to the Virgin Mary on the north side of the crossing. In the chapel opposite, Christ as the Good Shepherd is flanked by two angels. The one on his right is distinctly feminine in appearance; the other, a handsome male, has his sword swept back over his shoulder ready to smite the muscular devil trapped beneath his foot. Here, too, is one of the cathedral's most grotesque statues, that of St Bartholomew being flayed alive. Throughout the cathedral the floor is paved with slabs of white marble ornamented with geometrical patterns in red and black. And do not leave the interior without visiting the remains of the original fifth-century church with its well-preserved mosaic flooring and octagonal font. The fish-tail patterns in the tile- and brickwork here are the same as those in San Lorenzo and San Simpliciano (see p. 35), and are a clue to the original building's age.

Five centuries ago the piazza in front of the west door of the cathedral would have been both a meeting-place and a market. The present piazza, well over 1000 square metres in area, was designed by Giuseppe Mengoni in 1865. Today only flowers, toys, balloons, postcards and junk food are on sale, but this is still a place for political demonstrations, sporting activities and, most important of all, for people to congregate. At Christmas people of all ages and classes gather here. The air is heavy with the smell of roasting nuts and there is constant background music from wandering musicians. These perform in pairs. One plays a form of bagpipe (*cornamusa*) – basically a leather bag and chanter, though old prints show that these instruments were once more complicated. He also carries a drum and cymbals on his back, beating the former with a stick controlled by his elbow, the latter by a cord attached to one of his feet. His companion plays a reeded instrument like a primitive oboe (*piffero*), some of which have a surprisingly good tone. Often there are four or five pairs of these musicians in the piazza, their sound piercing the buzz of conversation as they wander about in front of the cathedral and in the adjoining streets. And around the north edge of the square art students produce large chalk pavement drawings of religious subjects. These often take more than a day to finish and at night are covered with sheets of polythene. Hats and plates are trustingly left for several hours for people to make contributions, and portable radios producing Mozart or recent pop successes add to the mix of sounds. Also on the north side and just to the west of the cathedral's main entrance is the Albergo Diurno Cobianchi. This is really nothing more than an unusually sumptuous public convenience with showers and rather splendid toilets, but there is also an old booking-hall where you can still buy tickets for local transport, and a series of travel agency kiosks. Most of the original nineteenth-

Emblems of Italy's commercial prosperity high above the marble floors and expensive cafés in the Galleria Vittorio Emanuele II.

century décor has been retained, with much wood and marble. Old notices and posters adorn the walls and you have the strong impression that you have momentarily stepped back into a completely different period.

In August, when many *milanesi* leave their city, there is a music and film festival for those who remain and for the tourists. A stage is erected just to the south of the cathedral, and once the worst of the day's heat has passed open-air concerts are given by professional foreign and Italian orchestras. Some of the city's more attractive courtyards also provide a setting for small chamber groups.

To the north of the cathedral, between Piazza del Duomo and Piazza della Scala, is a complex arcade of shops, the Galleria Vittorio Emanuele II. Built between 1865–77, this was also designed by Mengoni and was intended to symbolize the political and moral authority of the new kingdom of Italy, united under its first monarch. The arcades are in the form of a cross, with beautiful marble floors beneath an amazing barrel vault of glass and iron. Murals high up above the central intersection depict voluptuous ladies receiving gifts, for the most part from coloured gentlemen, symbols of Italy's growing prosperity. Old pictures show the arcades illuminated by gaslight – there were, it is said, 2000 gas jets in all – and full of animated groups. Little, other than the gas, appears to have changed. These arcades are the place for expensive cafés, jewellers, books and fashion shops. They are at their liveliest in the early evening, when groups of businessmen gather to argue and joke before leaving for home.

At the northern end you come out on to Piazza della Scala, with its central statue of Leonardo da Vinci surrounded by some of his pupils. The main building here is the opera house, but before visiting it spend a few minutes in Palazzo Marino beside the entrance to the *galleria*. The sixteenth-century *palazzo* is now the city hall, its magnificent plaster ceilings ruined by fluorescent strip lighting, but it is normally possible to see the huge inner courtyard adorned with an array of carved animal and human heads.

Going to a performance at La Scala is another matter, especially if it is the first night of an opera. Tickets are expensive, and unless you are lucky and know someone in an influential position or can book from abroad, they can be difficult to obtain. Stendhal claimed that the ladies of early nineteenth-century Milan had only to be wealthy and stupid to be seen at La Scala, and perhaps times have not altogether changed, but he also recognized that it was 'the best theatre in the world'. Mrs Piozzi, too, was much impressed, describing it as 'a beautiful theatre . . . the finest fabric raised in modern days'. In Stendhal's day La Scala was only fifty years old, having been inaugurated by a performance of Antonio Salieri's *Europa Riconosciuta* in August 1778. Since then it has seen the best of the world's operas and their interpreters.

Although you may not be fortunate enough to enjoy a performance here, a ticket to La Scala's museum allows you access to parts of the theatre and to one of the boxes. In the long gallery with its magnificent chandeliers on the first floor there is now a bar. There is also a bust of an unsmiling Toscanini, clearly disapproving of the social gatherings beneath him. The theatre was carefully reconstructed, following the design indicated by old prints, after the 1943 bombings. The auditorium itself, with room for nearly 3000 people, is of a regular horseshoe design, with six tiers of boxes centred on a sumptuous presidential or royal box two tiers deep. A huge chandelier is suspended from the domed roof and clusters of lamps elsewhere resemble the original gas lights. All is red, gilt and pale cream.

La Scala's museum contains just about everything to do with the theatre's musical history: instruments, busts of composers and conductors, manuscripts, pictures and general memorabilia (including some delightful nineteenth-century opera glasses). There is also a section displaying Etruscan and Roman masks and miniatures in stone and terracotta. But two figures

---

Leonardo da Vinci surrounded by pupils in Piazza della Scala, just opposite the theatre.

dominate: Toscanini, whose medals, awards and various batons surround his death mask and a plaster cast of his hands; and, in another room, Verdi, whose death mask still has some of his hair sticking to it.

This monument to Italian music-making is only a few minutes' walk by the aptly named Via Verdi from Italy's major art museum, the Pinacoteca di Brera. But take instead Via Filio Drammatici – glancing if possible at the superb panelled ceiling on the first floor of no. 8 adjoining La Scala – and head across Via dell'Orso and along Via Ciovasso into the pedestrian area which continues beyond the Brera. Like the larger traffic-free zone a little further east (see p. 40), it has been well restored; plaster walls have been washed in the traditional ochre, orange and deep yellow, and bare brick has been tastefully used. As might be expected, perhaps, antique dealers are prominent, but these have not driven out the workshop on the corner of Vie Ciovasso and Carmine, where heaps of dilapidated furniture bear little resemblance to the polished and expensive objects for sale in the nearby shops. The second of these two streets will lead you to Piazza Carmine and the splendid fifteenth-century church of the same name, where plain brick and stone pillars, pointed arches and plasterwork are offset by the heavily baroque chapel to the Virgin Mary flanked by black marble pillars on the south side of the choir. Clearly wealthy and well-supported, the church is in stark contrast to that standing at the junction of Vie Madonnina and Marco Formentini nearby, now shut, in a state of disrepair and with only a few traces of wall-paintings just to the left of the west door. This ecclesiastical contrast seems to reflect a social and economic divide as well. Via Madonnina with its picture-framers, antique dealers, clothes shops, chic hairdressers and bars in expensively restored interiors is self-evidently aimed at tourists and the wealthy *milanesi*. So too are similar developments in Via Fiori Chiari into which it runs. But a few minutes spent

---

The rose window in the church of San Carmine with its delicate tracery in terracotta.

San Carmine: the visitation of the Holy Spirit. In this beautifully appointed church, the simplicity of brick and plaster contrasts sharply with an ornate baroque chapel to the Virgin Mary.

---

exploring the area between Via Fiori Chiari and the main Via Pontaccio to the north will uncover a poorer and more dilapidated world on the outer edge of this pedestrian enclave where values are clearly different. The contrast is not peculiar to Milan, but it does, in places, seem particularly acute here.

Reality, whether glossy or sordid, is quickly forgotten in the Brera gallery less than 100 metres away to the east. The gallery is Italy's, and indeed one of Europe's, finest; given the richness of the collections, it is impossible to attempt any sort of overview. It is housed in a restored building completed for the Jesuits during the eighteenth century which stands on the site of a fourteenth-century monastery. A two-storey, double arcade of paired columns surrounds the central courtyard where Antonio Canova's statue of Napoleon as a Roman god greets visitors imperially. Most of the original collection, which dates from 1803, is due to the influence and persistence of the nineteenth-century painter Giuseppe Bossi, who persuaded the government to allow works from secularized religious institutions and churches to be deposited here, initially with the idea that they would be used in teaching. Subsequent contributions and purchases over the last 150 years have resulted in a collection which is very comprehensive but now too big for the space available. It is advisable, therefore, to check with the museum's office which rooms are open at any given time, especially if there are particular works you wish to see. There is nothing more frustrating than to find half the gallery closed, or to glimpse dozens of paintings stacked in store-rooms due to lack of hanging space.

Everyone has their favourite works in any art gallery. Two paintings which I find especially moving and noteworthy in the Brera are *Il Cristo Morto* by Andrea Mantegna and *Madonna in Trono* by Piero della Francesca (c.1410–92). Both are well known. The Mantegna is memorable not only for its depiction of harrowing sorrow, but also for the revolutionary use of perspective, with Christ's body viewed from below as though by someone standing at his feet, a technique that can be seen again in Mantegna's paintings in Mantua (see p.77). The della Francesca is much debated because of the ostrich egg suspended above the Virgin's head, generally held to mark the spatial centre of the composition. This work is a study in balance and harmony, but it is the eyes of the figures standing around Mary in the painting which I remember. Only those of one of the angels, the fourth from the right, look directly at you and demand your attention. The rest are set in contemplation of something unseen. And should you wish to study these – or other –

paintings with the aid of any of the many excellent catalogues, the Brera library is open to the public and is most welcoming.

From the gallery, continue north across the main road to the churches of San Marco (in a piazza of the same name) and, to the west, San Simpliciano. San Marco, which dates from the thirteenth century, is an attractive building, with an elegant campanile crowned with a small conical spire rising beside the crossing and numerous chapels – which aerial photographs show were added during the Middle Ages – flanking the south side of the nave. During the course of extensive restoration in the 1970s, a wall-painting in grey, black and white by Giovanni Battista, one of Leonardo's pupils, was discovered on the west side of the church and is now on view. The church is also significant for having been the venue for the first performance of Verdi's *Requiem* in 1873. In addition to the fresco by Battista, there are other, more colourful sixteenth-century paintings on the walls and ceilings of the chapels, in particular Paola Lomazzo's depiction of the glory of the angels and the death of Simon, and Bernardino da Fossano's scenes from the Old and New Testaments. The chapels also contain the tombs of notable medieval Milanese families. The effigies of Salvarino Aliprandi, a Christ-like figure shown blessing his family, and of Lanfranco Settala, clad in black, star-studded robes like a magician, are the most memorable.

Between San Marco and San Simpliciano is Via Solferino, once described to me by a Milan friend as the city's equivalent of London's Carnaby Street, though the art, furniture and dress shops seem to me to be infinitely superior and more attractive. It is certainly popular with the young, and especially with students from the art school at the Brera, and is a pleasant spot to sit with an ice-cream or self-indulgent cake and take stock of this attractive corner of Milan.

But once again, as in Via Fiori Chiari, there is a sudden change. Between Vie Solferino and San Simpliciano several smart, relatively modern apartment blocks are interspersed with poor housing. The area, like the church, is being restored, but it is not difficult to imagine what this and similar must have been like less than fifty years ago.

San Simpliciano is a large, sprawling church whose origins lie in the fourth century. The unfussy interior with its brick and stone pillars and plastered ceiling panels is, in my view, one of the most impressive in Milan. Remains of the early church still form part of the visible structure in the north transept and above the altar there is a magnificent early sixteenth-century fresco by Ambrogio Bergognone of the crowning of the Virgin Mary. There are two cloisters, but these can only be reached by way of a house now used as a kindergarten, at no. 6 Via Chiostri. Immediately behind the church to the north is a dirt football pitch. You have the impression – rightly – that this is a popular, working church. It is held dear by the *milanesi* themselves and on 29 May each year it is the scene of one of Milan's traditional ceremonies. Tradition has it that the Holy Roman Emperor Barbarossa was defeated in the Battle of Legnano on this day in 1176 with the aid of the spirits of three saints buried in the church – Martirius, Sisinius and Alexander – who joined the fighting in the form of three white doves. Today dozens of the birds are released in the adjoining piazza to commemorate the saints' assistance.

From San Simpliciano, head west to Castello Sforzesco with its park and gardens, pausing on the way to glance at the Piccolo Teatro. Due to be opened in the early 1990s, this modern concrete building seems out of place and sits unhappily at the southern end of elegant Via Legnano, a striking contrast to, for example, no. 28, with its ornate façade and inner garden.

The original fifteenth-century castle was largely demolished by Napoleon in 1800 and what remains owes its preservation to the intervention of the Lombardy authorities at the end of the last century. The castle has been well restored after bomb damage in 1943, but it is only possible to imagine the full scale of the fortress which, from 1450, became the home of the Visconti family and one of the most sumptuous of its kind in all Italy. It is a dominant, some say overpowering, building and is best appreciated from aerial

Assorted members of the Sforza family? Sculptural fragments on display in Castello Sforzesco.

photographs. Dumpy round towers, aggressive brickwork, a drawbridge and arrow slits are reminders of its military and turbulent past. The inner courtyards are less forbidding, though token lawns do little to relieve the essential bleakness. Only the cobbled Rochetta courtyard with its clean-cut arcades on three sides and bare plasterwork gives any suggestion of the elegance created by the Viscontis. Military austerity also typifies the interior, though there are some fine wall-paintings, in particular the anonymous portrayal of Christ crucified just inside the entrance from Piazza d'Armi, the former training-ground. There are also well-organized archaeological and military museums, and collections of ceramics and paintings. Amongst the works of art displayed here is Michelangelo's last, unfinished work, *La Pietà Rondanini*, so modern in feeling that it could almost have been sculpted by Rodin.

The 50-hectare park, Parco Sempione, behind the

35

castle was landscaped in an informal, English style around a small lake at the very end of the nineteenth century. It is popular with families and with business people, who picnic here in good weather. The original lawns may have deteriorated, but the clumps of mature chestnuts, oaks and beeches are magnificent. The land rises gently to the north, where an equestrian statue of Napoleon III was placed prominently on a high point in 1927. A jogging path around parts of the most northerly section of the park is punctuated with regular notices detailing supplementary exercises for stressed *milanesi*, while the less energetic can study a

Above **Courtyard, galleries and watchtower of Castello Sforzesco. The bleakness of medieval life is easily sensed here.**

Right **Vista along Corso Sempione through the Arco della Pace at the north-western end of the gardens behind Castello Sforzesco.**

large poster indicating the different species of birdlife to be found here. The paths are named after world-famous writers – Goethe, Racine and Shakespeare, for example – and on the south-western side is the Palazzo

dell'Arte, built in the 1930s, the site of a triennial exhibition of the decorative arts.

From Sforzesco back to the cathedral along Via Dante is only a fifteen-minute walk, or you can take a tram from the tree-shaded stop just opposite the main entrance. Alternatively, for a final – and different – experience, continue past the triumphal Arco di Pace on the northernmost edge of the park, a grandiose classical monument designed by Luigi Cagnola in honour of Napoleon in 1807 and rededicated in 1859 to Italian independence. Beyond it, around Via Paolo Sarpi, is a lively working-class and artisanal district with a number of wood- and leather-workers. Also, like the area around the main station, this is now a major and growing Chinese quarter. After the forbidding atmosphere of the *castello*, the warmth and intimacy here are refreshing.

The north-eastern segment of the old city can also be approached by way of the *galleria*. Instead of crossing Piazza della Scala, however, tack back behind the city hall, across Piazza San Fedele and into Via Omenoni (street of the giants). The *palazzo* of the same name belonged to the sixteenth-century court sculptor Leone Leoni, who was responsible for the *omenoni* – eight huge sculpted torsos with sad and pensive expressions – on the street façade. At the end of the street is Via Morone with the Palazzo Belgioioso, now a restaurant, and the delightful house where the novelist and poet Manzoni lived in the nineteenth century and which is now a museum, with its furniture and fittings as they were in his day, some illustrations from *I Promessi Sposi* and some manuscripts. A collection of a different sort can be seen in the barber's shop on the left just past Manzoni's house, which has a display of old haircutting and beard-trimming instruments. Italian coiffure has come a long way! Within a hundred metres is the main street named after Manzoni, which cuts up north-east towards the public gardens and the city's modern art gallery.

One of the pensive giants sculpted in the sixteenth century by Leone Leoni in Via Omenoni.

No. 12 Via Manzoni, originally built in the seventeenth century, is the Museo Poldi-Pezzoli, which the collector Gian Giacomo Poldi-Pezzoli bequeathed to the city with its contents – 'ad uso e beneficio pubblico' – in the last century. Despite considerable damage during World War II, the house has been restored and is a first-rate example of nineteenth-century Milanese elegance. The fine marble staircase with its wrought-iron balustrade, the baroque fountain, the plaster-work, carved panelling, inlaid furniture and highly-polished wood floors, and wall colours ranging from delicate pastels to dark, chocolate brown make the house as interesting as the works of art it contains. Of these, one painting, a fifteenth-century portrait of a lady in profile, is internationally famous, because no one knew who had painted it; it has now been attributed to Piero del Pollaiuolo. But there are some less well-known, amusing items. In what was probably originally the chapel, a late eighteenth-century Venetian porcelain figure depicts a merchant pleading honesty and innocence. His pot belly and pug-nosed face tell a different story.

Just beside the museum, set back from the road, is an arch crowned with a classical sculpture depicting a warrior (Achilles?) carrying off Astyanax, the son of Hector, whom Achilles has just killed in the Trojan war, while his imploring mother Andromache protests in vain. Beyond is an excellent example of the kind of internal garden with mature trees and classical statues that is hidden within so many of Milan's large houses. Another view of it can be had from a modern shopping arcade two entrances further down.

A matter of minutes takes you from the museum to the public gardens. Rather like those behind Castello Sforzesco, these would appear almost English in spring and autumn were it not for the statues and busts of celebrated Italians. Around the perimeter are the natural history museum, the city's principal modern art collection in the splendid neo-classical Villa Reale, the cinematographic museum in Palazzo Dugnani, which also boasts frescoes by Giovanni Tiepolo in the main room, and the zoo. All deserve to be visited. The modern art collection contains some fine nineteenth-

39

This figure on the Porta Venezia, one of Milan's several triumphal arches, seems to be in some doubt as to the benefits of conquest.

and twentieth-century works, especially by Modigliani, de Chirico, Picasso and the French Impressionists. The informal gardens provide welcome shade in summer, but they are at their best in early evening during the spring and autumn; mothers take their young children to play there and elegant *milanesi* stroll before the theatre or dinner. At the same time, despite patrolling policemen, they also provide shelter for groups of down-and-outs whose presence is a reminder of the darker side of the city's character.

From the eastern corner of the gardens turn back down the wide Corso Venezia, which contains a remarkably high proportion of large imposing *palazzi*. Almost opposite the natural history museum is the Palazzo Rocca-Saporiti, its neo-classical façade dominated by six Ionic columns and topped by eight classical statues. Further down on the other side of the road is the Palazzo Castiglioni of 1903, a complete contrast in style and arguably the finest *art nouveau* building in Milan. The windows of the first floor with their ornate sculptures of fruit, leaves and tumbling babies provide a welcome relief from the severity of some of the nearby architecture. And neo-classicism at its most severe is found at the Palazzo del Senato only 100 metres away. In mild weather shrubs in concrete tubs are placed symmetrically round the two interconnecting courtyards – the smaller surrounded by a two-storey colonnade – in an attempt to alleviate the general air of solemnity – but to little avail! The library, lecture rooms, studios and centre for Italian-Swiss cultural affairs now housed here echo the buildings' original function as the centre for diplomatic relations between Milan and Switzerland in the seventeenth century.

Once you have crossed Via Senato and re-entered the real hub of the city, the atmosphere changes abruptly. Virtually all this area, known as the Quadrilatero, is pedestrianized, beautifully kept and with a high percentage of expensive fashion and jewellery shops. The narrow streets are one of the cooler parts of the city in summer and around Christmas Via della Spiga is carpeted in red! But the modern commercial glossiness has not hidden several buildings and architectural features of note: the finely constructed brick backs to the shops in Via Borgospesso; the terracotta frieze work and three interconnecting courtyards in Via San Spirito; or the large arcaded entrance to what is now a clothes shop in Via Sant'Andrea, with its galleries of double arches dating from 1507. From here it is possible to cut through Via Bagutta – perhaps taking in the restaurant – to rejoin the main road in Piazza San Babila, surrounded by modern shopping arcades. Two very different churches face one another diagonally across the piazza: romanesque San Babila, small and intimate, and San Carlo al Corso, a grandiose mid nineteenth-century model of the Pantheon in Rome. From here Corso Vittorio Emanuele, rebuilt after World War II and popular with the young for its bars and cinemas, leads to the east end of the cathedral.

Tours of the southern half of central Milan can be

divided by Via Torino leading down to the Porta Ticinese and the canals, the Navigli Grande and Pavese. Constructed in the Middle Ages, these waterways became major routes for trade and communication, though Stendhal recorded that the journey to Venice via Pavia was subject to attacks by robbers and not to be recommended. Today luxury cruises on the Naviglio Grande as far as the Ticino National Park (see p.196) are less hazardous.

Immediately south of the cathedral is the cluster of buildings which includes the episcopal palace and the Palazzo Reale. The latter was originally Milan's medieval city hall and the palace of the Visconti dukes and was remodelled in its present neo-classical style in the eighteenth century. It now houses a museum with exhibits relating to the building of the cathedral, an art gallery, and some of the cathedral's treasures, including a wooden model of the building. Fittingly enough, it is all rather formal and grand, the *sala delle colonne* with a medusa-like design on a glass screen at one end being especially impressive – which is more than can be said for most of the pieces of renaissance sculpture displayed here.

If you walk through Palazzo Reale you come out by the fourteenth-century church of San Gottardo in Corte. Much of the original building has disappeared, but fortunately the exquisite octagonal seven-storey brick tower has survived. The whole edifice is trimmed with white stone and the top three stages are decorated with arches. The church is still used. It is a beautiful, intimate building and contains a fragment of a fresco depicting the Crucifixion that is attributed to one of Giotto's pupils. On the left is a quaint altar that looks as if it might once have been a chimney.

In my experience San Gottardo is unduly neglected by visitors to Milan. So too is San Satiro, directly west across Piazza Diaz. For years this church, the work of Donato Bramante (1444–1514), has been badly in need of internal restoration, the walls and ceiling blackened by the candle-smoke accompanying centuries of worship, but gradually the grime is being removed and by the early 1990s it should be possible to see it in all its renaissance splendour. Already the area around the

The elegant sweep of the monumental staircase in the Palazzo Reale di San Gottardo.

altar, and the cupola with its panels depicting golden roses on a green background, have been restored. This church is especially remarkable for the impression of space it conveys, due partly to its basic proportions, but more so to the illusion of an apse behind the high altar. To anyone standing in the nave, this appears to stretch back for at least three metres, but on close inspection it is seen to be less than a metre deep. Side panels painted as if seen on a curving wall and cleverly positioned pillars are responsible for this impression.

A third notable church in this area is the seventeenth-century Sant'Alessandro immediately to the south. It is extraordinarily ornate, a feast of decorated plaster and polished marble. The high altar, a row of reliquaries behind it, is studded with semi-precious stones and lavishly gilded, and the pulpit with its ornate canopy is also extravagantly decorated. Heavy carving marks the confessionals. Acoustically

41

the church is good and is used regularly for concerts, but there are other sounds here too. On the south side, directly beneath the church, is a locksmith's and chain-maker's, from which faint, disembodied voices can be heard through a ventilation grille covering what appears to have once been a well. On a late winter afternoon, when it is growing dark and the church is deserted, such noises can be quite disconcerting.

Less than a kilometre to the south-east of Sant' Alessandro is the state university, housed in a former hospital, the Ospedale Maggiore (backing on to Via Francesco Sforza). The main façade of the buildings – nearly 300 metres long – is impressive by any standards. The lower and earlier section dating from the fifteenth century is richly and beautifully decorated with window bays in carved terracotta; the later, northern end of the façade is seventeenth-century and much more severe. Inside there are three courtyards, each surrounded by two tiers of arcading. It is easy to imagine the building as a hospital, but today it throngs for much of the year with a large student population. Notices and posters announce everything from second-hand bicycles to class time-tables, from political meetings to visiting speakers. A small grassed area, Largo Richini, in front of the main entrance is packed in fine weather with groups of young people who spill over into the nearby cafés. The place has a most attractive atmosphere, agreeably free from the kind of sobriety which characterizes so much of central Milan. Student union offices at no. 26 in the adjoining Via Pantano look out on to a marble and stone arcaded courtyard, while no. 28 has an ornate top-floor balcony and decorated upper storeys. Only the ugly fuel tanks behind the shops facing Corso di Porta Romana are an eyesore.

Between the university and the Corso is one of Milan's most interesting churches, San Nazaro Maggiore, whose guardian priest will engage you in conversation for hours and press guidebooks into your hand given the slightest encouragement. Officially the first church on this site is said to have been founded by St Ambrose in 386, though a pillar at the entrance to the south crossing bears the date 382. The present building dates from the eleventh century, when the original church was severely damaged by fire, but has been much altered over the last hundred years. Its romanesque splendour has now been fully and expensively restored, with attractive ribs of brick and white marble crossing the plastered ceiling. A superb painting of the fourth station of the Cross dominates the north wall, and there is also a fourteenth-century fresco depicting the martyrdom of St Rita, with a striking dwarf portrayed in the left-hand panel, and a modern white marble sculpture by Pablo Atchugary of Christ being taken from the Cross. San Nazaro is best known for its main entrance, the octagonal funerary chapel designed by Bartolomeo Bramantino (c.1466–1536) for the powerful Trivulzio family, which had exerted considerable influence in local politics and business affairs during the previous century. The family's mortal remains are contained in marble sarcophagi in a series of niches high in the arches along the sides of the chapel. In the church of Les Invalides in Paris visitors have to look down – and therefore bow their heads in respect – to see Napoleon's tomb; here they are forced to look up in admiration. From the outside, the church with its jumble of roofs at different angles seems to wrap itself intimately around some neo-classical houses.

Before heading south for the Porta Ticinese, follow the path between San Nazaro and the university buildings and then Via San Barnaba past the new hospital and the law courts to the unusual early eighteenth-century Rotonda, formerly the site of a leper colony and of the hospital's cemetery. Today its classical colonnades are rather the worse for wear, but it is a safe place for young children to play and is popular with families, especially in spring and early summer. The original church in the middle, San

Alongside the Naviglio Grande, the waterway linking Milan to the Ticino. In sharp contrast to much of central Milan, this area is still authentically working-class, but ripe for development.

Michele, is in the form of a Greek cross. It is now deconsecrated and used occasionally for art exhibitions.

Walking diagonally south-west from here will quickly bring you to the Porta Ticinese in Piazza XXIV Maggio. Like the Arco di Pace to the north of Castello Sforzesco, this classical arch is the work of Cagnola; originally built to celebrate Napoleon's victory at Marengo in 1800, it was subsequently also dedicated to peace. It is worth taking an hour or two to explore the canal area round about. Parts are distinctly unattractive, with modern, uniform tenement buildings, pockets of industrial development and a mixture of cheap clothes shops, book-binders, mechanical workshops, dry-cleaners, pottery studios, health-food stores, bars and cafés lining the waterside, where some of the barges are floating bars and restaurants. Much is also in a poor state of repair. But just behind this façade you quickly get an idea of what Milan must have been like a hundred years ago. Narrow, part-cobbled streets, tiny courtyards, pretty balconies with potted plants, the occasional and unexpected tree, mysterious staircases, amateur wall-paintings and tributes to various saints provide character and interest. Children and cats appear from nowhere, dogs nose you suspiciously, the voices of people unseen reverberate from one building to another, smells of cooking drift appetizingly past.

This, for me, is Milan at its most authentic and attractive; a part of the city that is yet to be overtaken by modern commercialism. And it is a reminder too of the importance of the canals themselves in Milan's history. Conceived as early as the twelfth century, they were intended to form part of the city's defences and to provide a drainage system against the ever present threat of flooding. The earliest to be developed were the three major waterways linking Milan to the Adda, Ticino and Po: the Naviglio Grande running south-west to Abbiategrasso, the Naviglio della Martesana heading north-east to Canonica, and the Naviglio Pavese leading directly south. Subsequently, in the fifteenth century, the system was augmented with a number of smaller canals which connected with various suburbs and made it possible to circumnavigate the city. Old prints show this navigable route lying just outside the medieval walls. The canals' past glory is commemorated every year at the beginning of June by the colourful Festa dei Navigli, when the banks are lined with stalls and brightly painted boats strewn with flowers jostle for position. But they are not always so colourful and the slow-moving water is becoming increasingly polluted. I find them at their most attractive on a January or February afternoon; with snow on the ground and the surrounding buildings fading from grey to black with the light, their atmosphere is at the same time mysterious, bleak and historic.

Back across Piazza XXIV Maggio, where the Porta Ticinese dominates a bedlam of interweaving cars, buses and trams, is the basilica church of Sant' Eustorgio, with a fine front porch in pale sandstone and a soaring belfry tower. There has been a church on this site from the fourth century, but the building which evolved through modifications over the next 700 years was almost completely destroyed in 1164 by Frederick Barbarossa. The present, largely late thirteenth-century church is full of splendid plaster-work, monuments and paintings, among them Giovanni da Balduccio's ornate gothic tomb for Stefano Visconti (1327), the unfinished marble altar front, and the mid fifteenth-century chapel built for the Florentine banker Pigello Portinari by Michelozzo. This domed chamber is rightly considered one of Milan's greatest renaissance works. Around the dome are a rich stucco frieze and frescoes by Vincenzo Foppa which, amongst other things, depict scenes from the life of St Peter the Martyr to whom the chapel is dedicated. More incidents from the saint's life appear on Portinari's sarcophagus, which is supported by eight statues of the virtues. Above it is a pyramidal canopy decorated with figures symbolizing the heavenly hierarchy. But notice too the superb brick window-frame with its eight intricately carved bands in the last chapel on the south side, or the brick ribbing on the stone pillars. A sense of space reminiscent of San Simpliciano is created by a continuous nave and

The Emperor Constantine framed by Roman pillars
and the west door of San Lorenzo Maggiore.

chancel almost 75 metres long, and by the pillars of the
arcades on either side, which appear to incline slightly
outwards.

Only a short stroll away, through Parco delle
Basiliche beyond the apse, is San Lorenzo Maggiore,
one of the most important examples of Romano-
Christian building, some say, in northern Italy. The
row of sixteen columns forming a kind of screen in
front of the church was, probably, once part of a

Roman temple. Like so many of Milan's churches, San
Lorenzo was substantially altered in the sixteenth
century, though it has retained its original octagonal
shape. From the gardens to the south, with no soaring
tower to balance the composition, it appears rather
heavy and squat, dominated by the cupola designed in
1574 by Martino Basso. Some academics claim that the
ground-plan of the original church reflects byzantine
models, but the most striking feature from the earliest
years is the wall mosaic depicting Christ with his
disciples and the abduction of Elijah, still extraordinarily fresh even after 1500 years. In the same chapel is
a skeleton which is said to be the mortal remains of St

45

Aquiline, as well as parts of the church's foundations which are generally thought to have been requisitioned from a nearby Roman amphitheatre. Also of much interest, and rarely mentioned in guidebooks, is a wall-painting, a copy by one of Leonardo da Vinci's pupils of the master's depiction of the Last Supper in Santa Maria delle Grazie (see p. 50). Although the plaster base is slightly damaged, the delicate colours have been well preserved and the composition and general sense of movement suggest either that the student was particularly gifted, or that, in addition to his other extraordinary qualities, Leonardo was an inspiring teacher.

There is a pleasant walk back to Piazza del Duomo from here through a web of narrow streets running more or less parallel with Via Torino, with odd places for refreshment *en route*. What is interesting about this area is how quickly it changes. By the time you have reached Piazza Missori, for example, it is almost as though you are in a different city. Central Milan's largest popular district has been left behind.

West and south-west central Milan is the hub of the city's business and financial activities, best visited, as already suggested, in the early morning, when the scent of fresh coffee hangs in the air. A cluster of banks is grouped around Piazza Cordusio, among them the ornate and heavily carved Banca d'Italia, built just before World War I but looking at least forty years older. But the institutionalized financial transactions do not exclude all others. This is one of the areas where popular markets are held, with traders gathering early on Sunday mornings to bargain over stamps, coins and postcards. The atmosphere is lively but serious, and those with patience – and good fortune – can find relative bargains here. Nearby, in Piazza dei Mercanti, is the medieval town hall and corn exchange dating from the early thirteenth century. Although the façade is spoiled by several windows that have been concreted over, the simple lines of the brick-built exchange with its open colonnade where merchants traded can still be appreciated. Opposite is the black-and-white marble fourteenth-century Loggia degli Osii, where judicial matters were once decided, now a

bank. In the middle of the first floor is the small balcony from which edicts and sentences would once have been read. Threatening designs fill the decorative panels: an eagle clutching a headless animal in the centre is flanked by serpents with half-swallowed human figures projecting helplessly from their mouths. In medieval Milan, the piazza was the equivalent of the forum in Roman times. Today, it is a popular thoroughfare and meeting-place, and is also occasionally used for exhibitions and open-air concerts.

South-west from here is the Ambrosiana with its art gallery and world-famous library. The building was designed in the early seventeenth century for Cardinal Federigo Borromeo, who appears in Manzoni's *I Promessi Sposi* and whose statue stands in the garden. The light, airy and efficient library is a splendid place to read or write and is much used by people of all ages and for all purposes. Only the almost constant buzz of hushed conversations with the attendants is a distraction and, if this proves irritating, you can always find relief in the art gallery. The most celebrated of the collection of drawings and fifteenth- to eighteenth-century paintings is Raphael's group of debating scholars, the *Scuola d'Atene*, one of the studies for his *Stanza della Segnatura* cycle in the Vatican. Rather more amusing is a painting of the Virgin, *Madonna in Trono fra Santi*, by Bramantino, in which the composition of the main group is balanced not only by the body of a dead man on the left of the picture, but also by a huge dead frog on the right.

For all its artistic wealth, however, nothing in the Ambrosiana seems to me to match the anonymous wall-paintings in Palazzo Borromeo in the piazza of the same name. Although the original doorway has survived, this sixteenth-century house was almost entirely destroyed in 1943 and restoration work inside has been careful if limited. The frescoes are on the

Santa Maria Podone overlooking Piazza Borromeo. Directly opposite the church is Palazzo Borromeo with unique frescoes illustrating medieval domestic life.

ground floor of the inner building – now an architects' office – and you have to ask permission both to see and to photograph them, but the effort is undoubtedly worthwhile. They are usually described as illustrating the transition between late gothic and renaissance art, but this dry assessment conveys nothing of their fascination. The paintings are on three walls and tell the story of an afternoon visit to an elegant, probably aristocratic lady. The first panel depicts the arrival of friends (two women and two men); the second a walk across the garden, with the hostess carrying something that resembles a long club; the third a game of cards. The scenery and setting, the positioning of the figures and the attempts at perspective are obviously significant. But study the lady's eyes. While the other four are intent on their game, she gazes out of the picture, preoccupied, bored maybe, but for whatever reason completely cut off from the social activity around her.

Before leaving Piazza Borromeo, visit the ancient, tenth-century church of Santa Maria Podone directly opposite the *palazzo* to see two more paintings, both of which probably date from the fourteenth century when the church was much restored. The first, on the north-east side, creates the illusion of an angel opening and coming through a section of the wall. The other, on the same side of the church, depicting the Virgin Mary showing Christ to one of the Wise Men, portrays Our Lord as already mature enough to bless his visitor! It, too, is unusual, and is a good example of how false the painting of young children frequently was at that time.

Directly west from the piazza is the Catholic university of Milan, the war memorial to victims of World War I and the church of Sant'Ambrogio. Smaller and younger (1931) than its state equivalent, but hardly less elegant, incorporating as it does the double cloisters of the original monastery of Sant'Ambrogio, the Catholic university brings animation to this area. And in early December it is supplemented by the market and fair held to celebrate St Ambrose's feast day on the seventh. Known as the *Fiera degli obei, obei* (*obei* deriving from *Che belli*), it draws crowds from all over the city and turns Piazza Sant'Ambrogio and the streets around into a noisy, colourful enclave.

Other than the cathedral, Sant'Ambrogio is Milan's, if not Lombardy's, best-known church. The first church here, founded in 386, was built in the grounds of the palace from which the Roman Emperor Constantine issued his edict granting Christians the right to practise their religion without hindrance. Four centuries later the monastery was added, and 200 years after that there began a series of modifications to the church which resulted in the building as it exists today. The west façade is approached through the atrium, the Atrio detto di Ansperto, a sober but elegant paved area surrounded by arcades. The façade closing the inner end is formed of two tiers of arches, three of uniform height below bearing five classically simple shapes which decrease in size with the gentle slope of the roof. Two bell-towers dominate the building: the decorated and taller dei Canonici to the north; the plainer dei Monaci to the south.

The interior is similarly elegant. The nave is flanked by alternately wide and slender stone pillars which rise into arches trimmed with brick and beyond through a windowless clerestory to a plastered, vaulted ceiling. The church is full of treasures, all under the benevolent and welcoming gaze of a statue of Ambrose himself. The most sumptuous is the ninth-century golden high altar (*altere d'oro*), rich in carvings depicting scenes from the lives of Christ and Ambrose, and studded with precious and semi-precious stones. Carvings on the base of the pulpit are both dramatic and amusing: two-tailed mermaids grasp a fin in each hand; hunting scenes include a dog with someone's foot in its mouth, another catching a deer by the tail and apocryphal winged beasts. Beneath the pulpit is an equally ornately carved fourth-century sarcophagus, and in the crypt below a glass tomb contains the gloriously macabre robed and crowned skeletons of three saints, Ambrose, Gervase and Prostase. More artefacts can be seen in the church's museum.

Sant'Ambrogio is understandably popular: parties

Santa Maria delle Grazie, where Leonardo's celebrated fresco of the Last Supper is to be seen.

of tourists or schoolchildren are almost always present. Even so, its simplicity is paramount. Come here late at night under a full moon, when the floodlights have been switched off, and you soon have a sense of being in the heart of medieval Milan eight or nine centuries ago.

Leave the church and pass through the double gateway of the Pusterla di Sant'Ambrogio, past a hideous castellated building, and into Via San Vittore. Here you will find the technological museum, Il Museo della Scienza e della Tecnica, housed in what was once the monastery of Santa Maria delle Grazie. This is an ideal place for rainy days and energetic children. Bicycles, trains, clocks, all kinds of engines and generators, and the precursor of the modern type-writer are exhibited in bright, spacious halls. One gallery is devoted to Leonardo, whose self-portrait is reproduced in an engraving on a large glass screen at its entrance. Here numerous inventions anticipate our modern age, but only 500 metres to the north one of his most famous paintings celebrates the Christian faith. This is his fresco of the Last Supper in the Cenacolo Vinciano, the former monastery refectory, which took Leonardo two years (1495–7) to complete.

The techniques he used and the general dampness of the building have combined to make the work exceed-ingly fragile, and there are records of its becoming discoloured well within a hundred years of its com-pletion. Modern restoration techniques would appear at last to have come to terms with the problem, though the fresco remains highly delicate and the lighting in the refectory has to be carefully controlled. The scene depicts the Last Supper at the moment Christ an-nounces that one of the disciples will betray him, and is notable for Leonardo's studies of the psychological and emotional responses this devastating forecast provoked. As Goethe said: 'The whole party is in disarray.' The painting has also caused much debate – and admiration – in recent years for Leonardo's subtle handling of perspective. Covering the end wall of the refectory, the fresco appears to invite you into another room and into the countryside beyond. Although it is seen from below, so skilful is the use of angles you have the impression of being slightly *above* the scene.

Both outside the refectory and at the entrance you will be pestered to buy postcards and slides, but do not be distracted or dissuaded from visiting the rest of Santa Maria, one of Milan's most important renais-sance churches. The decoration is sumptuous, with much carved marble and painting, but it is the apse designed by Leonardo's friend Bramante that is most impressive. Built over almost exactly the same period as it took Leonardo to execute his fresco, it is basically a huge cube topped by an arcaded cupola which many describe as a giant wheel. The apse completely dwarfs the main nave of the church, but viewed from any angle it demonstrates perfect architectural balance. Every detail – friezes, panels, medallions, windows and blind arches – contributes significantly to the overall effect. It is almost as though Bramante and Leonardo were, each in his own medium, vying to see who could produce a work with the highest degree of geometrical subtlety.

Leave Santa Maria to the south and turn east along Corso Magenta. On the north side is the baroque façade of Palazzo Litta, whose sumptuous interior includes a hall of mirrors with a beautiful inlaid floor of mixed hardwoods, crystal chandeliers and gilt carving. Opposite is the sixteenth-century Monastero Mag-giore, where many of the frescoes completely covering the interior of the church are by one of Leonardo's best-known pupils, Bernadino Luini. To him is attri-buted a series depicting the life of St Catherine of Alexandria, who survived her ordeal on the spiked wheel, only to be beheaded. Tradition has it that the figure of the saint was modelled on a local lady, Bianca Maria di Challant, who was herself beheaded in Milan in 1526.

Just next to the church is an archaeological museum and in the garden behind are the best-preserved remains of the third-century Roman fortifications of the city. More ruins can be seen in Via Ansperto nearby, where those responsible for the restoration of the medieval church here would seem to be faced with a well-nigh impossible task. This whole area, in fact, is yet another of the many throughout Milan where some

This muscular winged tribute to Mussolini is only one
of many which decorate Milan's Stazione Centrale.

restoration has taken place, but where many residential blocks are in a poor state of repair – externally at least. Were it not for the occasional chic roof-garden or tiny shop selling expensive glass and jewellery, you might think you were in some remote Lombardy village. Curiously, it is here that I found one of the most unprepossessing but expensive wine shops anywhere, where a bottle of 1961 Barolo could be had, I was told, for the modest sum of 800,000 lire. The 1937 vintage would have set me back 4,400,000 lire. Perhaps some of those who work around Piazza di Affari now only 200 metres or so away can – and do – afford such prices.

These selective tours do no more than scratch the surface of what can be seen in central Milan. Tiny churches, covered markets, courtyards glimpsed through half-open doors, elegantly simple town-houses, shady gardens, alleys and tiny *piazzi* tucked away off the main streets are a constant source of surprise and pleasure. Pockets of residential quiet will unexpectedly give way to areas dominated by the glass and marble of modern offices, or to others still reminiscent either of Milan nearly a century ago or of a genuine village community. And this is only the nucleus of a very large city. Unless time is virtually unlimited, it would not be realistic to attempt to explore areas further afield, though the modern underground system is both swift and efficient. Whatever the difficulties, however, no visit to Milan would be complete without some time spent in the Stazione Centrale or the Cimitero Monumentale.

Few European towns have a railway station of such ornamentation and dimensions to welcome its visitors. Although planned before World War I, it was only finished, as a tribute to Mussolini, in the early 1930s; it is the biggest railway station in Italy. Its ticket hall with a marble mosaic floor is like some huge temple, from which stairs and escalators ascend through one of three huge, gaping arches topped by friezes depicting Roman triumphs as though passing to another kingdom. The platforms stretch away for nearly 350 metres under a vast steel and glass canopy. As in most popular and busy stations with international connections, you soon find yourself somehow outside the normal preoccupations and routine of daily life – even if the problems presented by timetables are often more critical here than elsewhere!

A similar sense of timelessness is found in the cemetery. Designed *in stile lombardo moderno* in the mid nineteenth century by Carlo Maciachini, it is two kilometres away to the west, slightly bigger than the public gardens and about the same size as the main park behind Castello Sforzesco. Inside the main gates a mausoleum surrounding a large courtyard is a labyrinth of passages lined with marble boxes, together containing the mortal remains of tens of thousands of *milanesi*. Some are tiny, no more than 30 centimetres square, some record full family details, some only a name and date of decease, and others again the bleak anonymity of a mere 'occupation'. Above is a kind of pantheon decorated with scenes from Milan's history and with busts of local dignitaries. In the middle is the tomb of Alessandro Manzoni.

Outside, the grounds are immaculately kept. Yew and laurel trees and box hedges are neatly trimmed; the grass and pathways are weed-free and raked by a small army of gardeners. But what makes the cemetery internationally famous and truly justifies its description of *monumentale* is the variety of tombs. Every conceivable motif, biblical allusion and style are to be seen. Some chapels built of brick and tile resemble small conventional houses; others in marble, steel and plate glass are startlingly modern. Many tombs are modest in size; others are huge and incorporate grottoes, or massive animals, or abstract designs. Statues display every shade of emotion – terror, compassion, sadness, stoicism. One monument to a former actress depicts her skeleton clad in a shroud with a head radiant with former beauty in its left hand. Certain areas are 'reserved' for Protestants, Jews and Chinese, and there are collective monuments to those who died in World Wars I and II, or who perished in

The mausoleum in Milan's main cemetery has an oddly Moorish quality.

53

concentration camps. There could be no better reminder of the importance of religion to the Italian people, and as an open-air museum of tomb architecture the cemetery must also rank very highly with anywhere else in the world.

Until the early nineteenth century, Milan's dead were buried in medieval fashion in a series of cemeteries, each of which was situated just beyond one of the main gates to the city, but urban development, and the realization that the upper classes were not alone in demanding the right to a proper and dignified burial, led to the establishment of the Cimitero Monumentale. Now adjoining the commercial railway yards of the Stazione Porta Garibaldi and the city's permanent fairground, the Luna Park, it may not seem the most restful of places today. But go there late on a winter's afternoon with the sun sinking behind the mausoleum and with the mist beginning to rise from the damp soil and the buzz of Italy's brashest and most modern city will seem far away.

Opposite page and left **Designed in the mid nineteenth century by Carlo Maciachini, the Cimitero Monumentale is one of the finest museums of tomb architecture in the world, with a wealth of elaborate tomb decoration.**

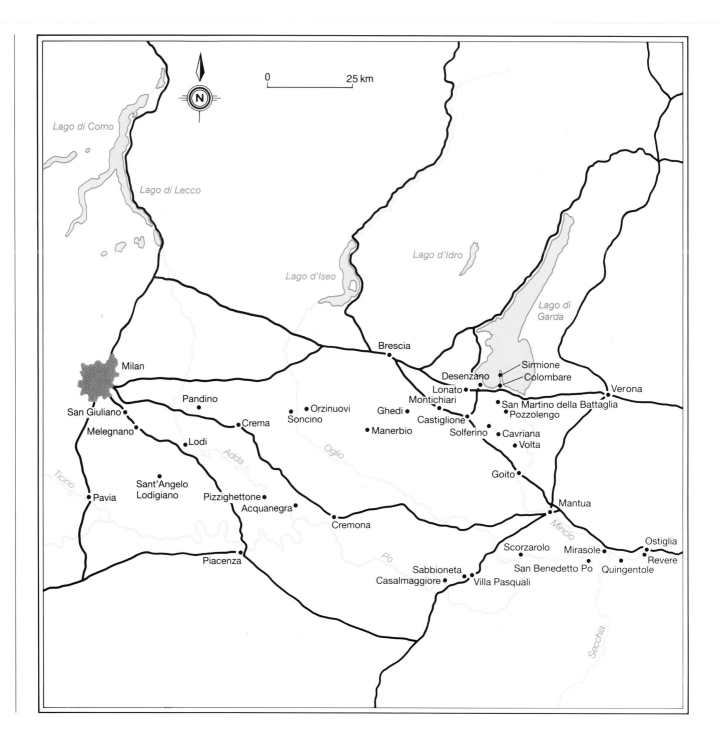

2
The Flat Lands

Lodi – Cremona – Casalmaggiore – Sabbioneta – Mantua –
San Benedetto Po – Solferino – Lake Garda – Sirmione –
Montichiari – Crema

Apart from the lakes, the best-known natural feature of Lombardy is undoubtedly the Po valley, with the river itself forming the region's southern boundary for much of its length. The Po is Italy's longest river, flowing east for 652 kilometres to the Adriatic Sea from its source in the western Italian Alps. It is joined by the Ticino, Adda, Oglio and Mincio, Lombardy's other major rivers. The valley is a vast fertile plain, in many places well over 50 kilometres wide, drained by a complex system of channels and ditches linking with the rivers and their smaller tributaries and intensively farmed. In summer it can be hot and humid, in winter desolate and windswept. But it offers magnificent skyscapes and on crisp, clear days the view north to the mountains of the Valtellina and the Alps beyond can be spectacular.

Despite modern roads, the impression created by many of the towns and villages is one of isolation, of communities which originally settled on areas of high ground away from the immediate danger of floods. The most convenient way to explore the region is by following the principal routes linking these communities, branching off on to secondary roads wherever possible. These may lead to a modern farm complex or to a medieval castle – either is typical of the Po valley.

A number of major routes run down and across the valley, among them the A1 motorway striking south-east out of Milan. Although there is nothing attractive about the city's industrial suburbs, and the military establishment at San Giuliano, it is preferable to take the parallel S9. A few minutes after the major junction at Melegnano, you get a view of Lodi, the main city of this area, situated on the Adda. Just to the east is Lodi Vecchio, the original Roman town strategically placed to control river traffic.

During the early Middle Ages the city was a rival to Milan and was destroyed in 1111 by the Milanese army. Forty years later the remaining population appealed to the Holy Roman Emperor Barbarossa for help and he, seeing Lodi as a potential ally in his struggle to gain mastery of northern Italy, founded the present-day town. Gratitude was short-lived, however, and Lodi joined the Lombard League as soon as Barbarossa had returned to Germany.

As you approach Lodi today it is not immediately attractive, its outskirts marked by light industry and new housing developments catering for Milan commuters. But the heart of the medieval town around the cathedral is splendid. To the east is Piazza di Mercato where one of the best markets of the region is held, its cheese stalls being especially memorable. To the west is the expansive, arcaded Piazza della Vittoria, lined

Above **Church, poplars and tilled soil combine in a characteristic landscape in the Po valley to the west of Casalmaggiore.**

Right **Windows overlooking Piazza di Mercato, Lodi. One of the best markets in the whole region is held in the square.**

with cafés and shops, those in Corso Roma expensive enough to remind you that this is not just a simple market town.

Dating from the twelfth century, the cathedral was completely and beautifully restored in the early 1960s. Its west front rises above Piazza della Vittoria, with a pair of pink marble lions carrying the two slender pillars which support the canopy of the main entrance. The massive studded wooden doors are flanked by effigies of a sleeping Adam and Eve. Inside, rich blues, greens and reds in the many frescoes dating from the thirteenth to the fifteenth centuries are now bright and clear, and crosses, chalices and other treasures from all periods are proudly displayed. The ornate reliquary altar at the end of the north aisle in particular should not be missed. Adam and Eve reappear in an amusing carving on the south side of the nave (on the second pillar from the west end), in which Eve looks beguilingly submissive. Beneath the high altar is the entrance to two crypts. One contains the tombs of Lodi's archbishops. The other has frescoes of St Anthony and of the Crucifixion which have been rubbed bare in places by the hands of the faithful, and a fine group of seven fifteenth-century wooden figures depicting the entombment of Christ, including a poignantly grief-stricken Virgin Mary.

Quite different in character is the richly ornate La Incoronata just north-west of the cathedral. This church was designed by Giovanni Battagio, one of Bramante's pupils, and though he quarrelled with the city council and resigned the commission, his plans were executed. Building was begun in 1488 and the church is Lodi's finest piece of renaissance architecture. It is a domed octagon with a gallery running round the outside of the dome. Two bell-towers were intended, but only one constructed. Inside, it is richly painted, four works by Bergognone depicting the Annunciation and scenes from Christ's life being particularly notable. So sumptuous is La Incoronata

Complaining lions bear the full weight of the canopy outside the west door to the cathedral in Lodi.

that it tends to outshine San Francesco only a few hundred metres further east. The unfinished, rather scruffy west front of this twelfth-century church gives no clue, however, to the mass of brilliant frescoes inside, originally sponsored by various local dignitaries and wealthy families. Scenes from the life of St Bernard completely cover a chapel on the south side; pillars in the nave bear frescoes of saints, St Catherine for some reason being allowed two appearances, while the Virgin, just inside the west door, is shown obviously and unflatteringly pregnant despite the child in her arms.

Just opposite this church, the cloisters of the fifteenth-century Ospedale Maggiore have largely preserved their original character, despite having been incorporated in the modern hospital and much restored. They are certainly worth a visit, but you need to ask permission at the main entrance.

From Lodi, head south-west to visit Sant'Angelo Lodigiano, with its Visconti castle overlooking the main square. This huge fourteenth-century fortress, dominated by its watch-tower, imposes itself on both the town and the surrounding area. Thoroughly restored early in the twentieth century, it is now a museum housing an important collection of books, arms and fifteenth- and sixteenth-century furniture. Unexpectedly, it is also the national bread museum, with a series of tableaux on the first floor illustrating the history of bread-making in Italy from the earliest, most primitive methods of mixing and baking to modern forms of production.

Beyond Lodi, about 20 kilometres downstream, Pizzighettone marks another fortified bridging-point. Although there are traces of earlier work, the surviving parts of the town wall date from the sixteenth century and are altogether less impressive than those at Sant'Angelo Lodigiano. From here, minor roads follow the Adda as it winds south to Cremona past the sinisterly-named village of Acquanegra ('black water'), a bleak place indeed in the depths of winter. Alternatively, Cremona can easily be reached from Sant'Angelo within half an hour by joining the S234 from Pavia.

Above **A fine example of typical Lombard brickwork and ornamentation at Sant'Angelo Lodigiano.**

Right **The castellated Torrione at Pizzighettone dominates the Adda. The campanile in the background provides an interesting contrast.**

The art of violin making, as taught at Cremona's famous school, has changed little since the time of Stradivarius.

Evidence has been found at Cremona of settlement by a Gallic tribe, the Cenomani, who were defeated by the Romans in 218 BC, but it was as a Roman city that the town first prospered. It was an important crossing point on the Po, and from these early years until the late Middle Ages was a natural junction for routes from Milan, Venice, Brescia and Piacenza. Like those of Lodi, its inhabitants sided with Barbarossa against Milan and even resisted the Lombard League for a while before eventually falling to the Viscontis in the fourteenth century. Both walled and moated, it was relatively secure, enjoyed patronage of the highest order and became a fashionable and much sought-after place of residence among wealthy medieval merchant families.

Today, Cremona is most widely known for its school where students are taught how to make stringed instruments. Housed in the late fifteenth-century Palazzo Raimondi, it was inaugurated in 1938 after the bicentennial celebration of the death of Stradivarius, one of the great instrument makers who worked in Cremona in the past. The annual intake of thirty students – fifteen from Italy, fifteen from abroad – is trained for five years here.

Italians enter at thirteen or fourteen and continue their studies in major academic subjects at the same time as they learn their craft. None the less, they are qualified before the age of twenty. Foreign students are almost always older, having studied elsewhere, and there is a policy of accepting them from countries where similar institutions do not exist in an attempt to spread the skills more widely. The only necessary requirements are relative youth and a good knowledge of Italian (tested by an entrance examination). On the face of it, such a policy seems enlightened. But each year approximately thirty newly-qualified instrument makers appear on a market-place that is already crowded. And there are others, too, who have dropped out or who have simply come to Cremona with dubious credentials. Once in possession of a basic diploma, anyone can set up in business, though the best usually continue to work (and study) with their teacher for up to ten years after they have received their final qualification. Thereafter success depends on skill, reputation and luck. Interestingly, if the present trend continues, by the end of the twentieth century at least 90 per cent of the instruments made in Cremona will find their way to Japan.

Inevitably, this community is rife with problems and jealousies, some of which may emerge if you find your way into one of the workshops. Several of the registered makers on a list provided by the local tourist office speak English and the experience can be rewarding. If you are fortunate you will see an instrument in the process of being made, and there is nothing quite like a naked, raw-wood violin or 'cello body to make you realize the work that goes into producing the highly polished object you see on the concert platform. It is also possible – if you can provide a good reason – to visit the school itself. The intensity and concentration of the dozen or so young people in each of the workrooms can almost be felt as they learn their highly delicate and technical trade. And rarely will you have seen such an array of chisels, scrapers, clips, saws, glues and sandpaper.

Curiously enough, such productivity appears to end with the instruments themselves. Amateur or semi-professional music-making in Italy may not be as vigorous as it is in Britain, but it does seem odd that there should be no resident Cremona orchestra and relatively few concerts given by local musicians.

The modern school at Cremona is only the most recent expression of a very long tradition. Examples of instruments made by the Amati family (who flourished from the sixteenth to the eighteenth century), Giuseppe Guarneri 'del Gesù' (*fl*.1725–45), Antonio Stradivari (*c*.1644–1737) and other great makers of the past who worked here can be seen in the thirteenth-century Palazzo del Comune, opposite the cathedral. The remarkable collection shown in the Saletta dei Violini includes three violins of particular note. First, there is the instrument made in 1566 by Andrea Amati (1505–80) for Charles IX of France. The Amati family – Andrea, Giovanni and their father, Gottardo – were the first major violin makers in Cremona. This particular instrument, extensively restored in 1818, has an amazingly rich tone and, despite wear, bears traces of its original ornamentation. On the back, cut from a single piece of maple, are parts of the inlay work which bore Charles' personal emblem and the remains of a Latin inscription can be seen on the sides. The front is made up of two pieces of spruce and the whole instrument is varnished in a deep brown-orange which brings out the grain and flare of the woods to their best advantage. There is also a violin by Andrea's grandson Nicolo (1596–1684), the best known, most versatile and, financially, probably the most successful of the Amati dynasty. His instrument is known as the Hammerle, after the collector Teodor Hammerle. It is claimed that the varnish is original and it seems probable that the violin has undergone less restoration than Andrea's instrument. It is marginally bigger and is of a beautiful golden orange colour which is characteristic of his work. The third violin is by Nicolo Amati's most famous pupil, Antonio Stradivari who succeeded him as the finest violin-maker in Italy. It contains an original label bearing the date 1715, the year universally considered to be his best and when he produced at least ten violins of similar quality. It is not known who the first owner was, but in 1889 the instrument belonged to the great violinist Joseph Joachim (1831–1907). For this reason it is known as 'Il Cremonese ex Joachim del 1715'. Fractionally bigger again than Amati's instrument, it produces a deep, mellow sound, especially from the G string. It too is a lovely golden orange in colour and is claimed to have its original varnish.

Seen together in their atmospherically-controlled glass cases, these and other violins are a moving and beautiful testament to a truly great period of stringed instrument making, some of whose secrets have still to be discovered. But even more exciting is to hear them. In order to keep these violins 'alive', they are taken out of their atmospherically-controlled glass cases every morning and played.

On the same floor as the Saletta dei Violini is a series of rooms filled with furniture, decorations and paintings, the many interesting pieces here including a beautifully and delicately carved marble chimney-piece in the Sala della Giunta, and a life-size plaster model of the marble Porta Stanga, the doorway carved in 1490 for the Stanga family's *palazzo* in Corso Garibaldi which is now in the Louvre in Paris. This replica leads into the council chamber, the Sala del Consiglio, where I was struck by two paintings in particular. Luigi Miradori's *La Moltiplicazione dei Pani* (1647) is an attempt at perspective which unfortunately resulted in a huge naked child at its mother's breast in the foreground. And the figure being roasted alive in the *Martyrdom of St Lawrence* seems supremely oblivious to his pain and of little interest to several of his tormentors or the onlookers.

There is a fine view of the Palazzo del Comune from the thirteenth-century Torazzo tower across the square to the north of the cathedral. Approximately 112 metres high (the figure varies according to which

65

source you consult), the tower is open every day and those with a head for heights can enjoy magnificent views over the roofs of Cremona and the surrounding plain. Now the symbol of the town, the tower is built of brick, six storeys high, and topped with two marble octagonal and arcaded galleries. An astrological clock on the west façade is original, but the bronze lion which once sat on the pinnacle of the campanile has been replaced by a gilded ball and a cross.

The whole complex of buildings around Piazza del Comune is completed by the cathedral and twelfth-century baptistery. The latter, much restored in the sixteenth century, is an octagonal building with a monumental font of 1530 by the sculptor Leonardo Trotti and three altars, none of which is especially distinguished. The eight brickwork panels making up the vaulted roof, however, are quite breathtaking, the knowledge of mathematics and engineering skills which they demonstrate nothing less than awe-inspiring.

The same kind of response is solicited by the cathedral. Also begun in the twelfth century (though not completed for another 200 years), it is one of the finest examples of romanesque architecture in Lombardy. As at Lodi, the pillars supporting the canopy above the west door are carried on two complaining pink marble lions. Arcades spill across the façade on either side, with two dwarf galleries and a large rose window above them. A wealth of carved stone includes a tablet to the left of the west door depicting the Temptation, with Adam and Eve in coy poses, while the frieze above the door illustrates the yearly round of agricultural tasks, such as ploughing, harvesting and woodcutting.

Inside, despite the relative lack of natural light, the entire building is a mass of colour from the paintings covering most of the walls. Scenes from Christ's life above the arches along the north side of the nave and

Palazzo del Comune, Cremona. Behind these windows are some of the world's rarest and most valuable violins.

several opposite of the Stations of the Cross by Giovanni de Pordenone (1483–1539) repay close attention. Also striking, but in a different way, is a painting of the Crucifixion beneath the west window, with figures in sixteenth-century dress. In the foreground a knight holding a huge sword in his right hand points back at Christ with his left; the symbol of militant Christianity is unambiguous. And of the chapels, the most impressive is just to the left inside the west door. Dedicated to the Virgin, it is dominated by a painting of Our Lady flanked by four twisted black marble columns decorated with gilt leaf motifs. Above them, two soaring cherubs hold her crown and the whole composition is covered by a richly baroque gilt canopy. Only the intrusive electric candles detract from the chapel's powerful appeal.

Delightful warrens of narrow streets radiating out from this impressive central complex hide other notable churches and splendid *palazzi*. The eleventh-century Santa Agata in Corso Garibaldi contains Gian Cristoforo Romano's mausoleum of 1502 for the Trecchi family, one of the wealthiest and most influential in fifteenth-century Cremona. The church also has some splendid modern mosaics (1968) and stained glass (1928), as well as sixteenth-century frescoes by Giulio Campi depicting scenes from the life of St Agatha. Part of her hideous martyrdom involved having her breasts cut off. Not far away, the fourteenth-century church of Sant'Agostino in the piazza of the same name is notable for its ceiling paintings by Bonifacio Bembo dating from 1452. Those representing the Evangelists and the Wise Men of the Church (in the third chapel from the west end on the south side) portray the good doctors as both miserable and uncomprehending! In the adjacent chapel is a most brutal eighteenth-century sculpture of the Stations of the Cross.

In addition to these two churches, look out for the sixteenth-century Santa Margherita in Via Trecchia and the slightly older Santa Maria Maddalena, diagonally across town in Via XI Febbraio. The former is a popular church but has not enjoyed the kind of financial support received by Sant'Agostino which, despite the bushes visible on the roof today, was

Left There is something vaguely oriental about this medieval juggler – or sportsman – from Cremona, who also seems to be in danger of losing his trousers.

Above Cremona has one of Lombardy's several astrological clocks; others can be seen at Brescia and Clusone.

69

totally renovated in the early 1950s. Santa Margherita's decorations are threatened by damp and those responsible for the church have had to resort to ugly electric heaters to alleviate the problem. Damp also threatens Santa Maria Maddalena. Dating from the fifteenth century, and on the site of an older church, it is interestingly skewed, with its high altar nearly directly south, something you sense as soon as you walk in. Among the frescoes here is one of the Adoration of the Magi depicted with a delicacy worthy of Bembo. You will also see the body of St Gerald in a glass case. But it was the worn stone slabs paving the main north entrance which moved me most in this tiny building. Most Italian churches give the impression of being well used, but there is a particularly strong feeling here of the tens of thousands of the faithful who have passed through this door over the centuries.

The *palazzi*, several of which are privately owned or have been acquired by national institutions, are not always so accessible. The sumptuous interior of Palazzo Stanga Trecca opposite San Lorenzo in Via Palesto, for example, includes the bedroom reserved for Napoleon, with scenes of imperial Roman victories and a magnificent canopied bed. But it can only be seen with the permission of *il presidente* of the Istituto Tecnico Agrario, and he resides in Milan! But at least you can visit the courtyard and see the exquisite arcading and terracotta carvings of battle scenes, classical figures and flower motifs. Palazzo Fodri, in Corso Matteotti, is now owned by the Banca d'Italia. In some ways this is fitting, since it was built at the very end of the fifteenth century for a wealthy merchant, Benedetto Fodri, at a time of expansion and prosperity in Cremona's history. A century later, the house was sold to the Church and became a monastery until 1784. The entrance porch has some interesting fifteenth-century fresco-work by Antonio della Corno, including classical motifs and monochrome portraits of

Roman emperors, while the arcaded and galleried courtyard conveys a real sense of late medieval Cremona. In all this is one of the most attractive of the town's *palazzi*; that the monks were reluctant to leave its comforts is hardly surprising.

Such was Cremona's former wealth that little gems of town houses can be found at almost every turn. No. 26 in Via Palastro, for example, has a brick and terracotta façade; at no. 10 in Via Bertesi, not far away, well-trimmed lawns are set off with classical statues. On a smaller, more intimate scale is no. 18 in Via Beltrami off Piazza della Pace, now transformed into offices. Rarely will a street, however tiny, not contain a house of some distinction. Today Cremona is once again a prosperous, thriving community, but this prosperity is relatively recent. On my last visit to the town I was fortunate to see an exhibition of photographs taken mainly in the twenties and thirties which depicted rural and urban trades and occupations. One picture in particular remains fresh in my mind. Two women prepare fruit and vegetables for market, their hands bare despite the piles of snow all around. In the background a cyclist buys a hot drink from a small hut, one side of which is plastered with an advertisement for Coca Cola showing a young, smiling couple in party clothes. The contrast is stark: the photograph is worthy of Bill Brandt.

Winter in Cremona can be cold, and signs of life soon disappear from the streets, but in spring and summer voices will seep out between half-closed shutters. And even in this curiously unmusical town, there will be the occasional sound of a piano. As you depart, notice how quickly the old town refuses to follow. The ring road has been built on the line of the original moat; once across it, you are into modern development which could be suburbia anywhere.

Leave Cremona by any of the minor roads which wander down river through a series of small settlements clustered on islands of high ground above what were periodically flooded areas along the Po. Suburbia quickly gives way to a vast agricultural plain which spreads 100 kilometres east, beyond Mantua, to the eastern border of Lombardy. This immensely fertile,

---

Cremona, façade of Santa Agata: St Agatha about to undergo her martyrdom at the hands of the Romans.

silt-rich valley is largely arable land, but it also supports some cattle and areas of orchards. Occasional rows of vines like tall green fences seem to be acting as barriers or lines of demarcation rather than anything else. The soil is of a warm brown colour and the fields are often surrounded by irrigation channels. Many of the farmsteads are in the *cascina* style, but, despite obvious signs of wealth, are often in need of attention. Once off the main roads, you will often find yourself on dirt or gravel tracks, but these are adequately made and allow you to cut back and forth across the area.

Casalmaggiore overlooking a bridge across the Po is a sizeable, sprawling village with a lively Saturday market in the square fronting the castellated town hall and in the adjacent streets. A restored brick house and an elegant sixteenth-century building with shops accommodated on the ground floor grace Piazza Turati behind the town hall. Nearby, on the corner of Via Chiozzi, is an example of one-time arcaded splendour that is in danger of being lost if a benefactor is not found soon. Also visit the huge seventeenth-century church with its galleried choir and striking modern sculpture of Christ with arms upstretched.

About 5 kilometres north-east on the Mantua road is Sabbioneta, a tiny walled village rightly considered one of the jewels of eastern Lombardy. Two gates — Porta della Vittoria on the west and Porta Imperiale on the east — lead through the ramparts. The village was designed in the sixteenth century by Vespasiano Gonzaga in an attempt to realize the renaissance conception of an ideal city, accommodating about a thousand people. It took forty years to complete. Inside its irregular hexagonal walls, the streets are laid out in the form of a subtly distorted grid focused on two squares, Piazza d'Armi and Piazza Ducale, an architectural reflection of the Gonzaga family emblem, which is a labyrinth. Sabbioneta quickly became known as *piccola Atene*, 'little Athens', a fitting name for a town containing one of Italy's most important

theatres, Il Teatro Olimpico, designed by Vincenzo Scamozzi in 1588–90, restored in 1950, and still regularly used for productions every September. At its eastern end there is a raised colonnade topped by a dozen figures of classical gods which curves elegantly round the rectangular and slightly sunken auditorium. Up to two hundred people can be comfortably seated here and it is not difficult to conjure up a picture of the audience that would have enjoyed performances hundreds of years ago.

When nothing is being staged here, the theatre can only be seen on application to the tourist office; so too can the other major historical buildings, of which three in particular should be sampled. The first is the Palazzo Ducale, designed by Paolo and Bassano Tusardi and built in 1568, where four wooden and plaster statues of members of the Gonzaga family show them as knights on horseback (originally there were twelve). The second is the Galleria degli Antichi, built in the same year, to the south of the town. This is a 100-metre long arcade with a first-floor gallery and rooms decorated with frescoes depicting mythological scenes, the most notable of them by Bernardino Campi. There is also a room full of mirrors and pastoral scenes by the same artist which once contained a collection of Roman busts, but these are now in the ducal palace in Mantua. Finally, there is the sixteenth-century church of the Incoronata, behind the ducal palace, where Vespasiano Gonzaga is depicted in bronze as a Roman emperor by Leone Leoni and his mausoleum is richly carved by G. B. della Porta.

The heart of Sabbioneta is seen to best advantage in bright light, when the marble of the façade of the Palazzo Ducale glows subtly pink and the pastel colours of plaster walls show to good effect. Particularly rewarding, too, is a stroll through the streets in the middle of the day in summer, when most people are indoors. But it is also impressive on a misty day in autumn or winter, when it seems deserted and completely cut off from the outside world.

Just outside the village on the Mantua road is the hamlet of Villa Pasquali, where both the imposing baroque Chiesa del Bibiena and the cemetery —

A mildly erotic tribute to the Gonzaga family in the ducal palace in Sabbioneta.

probably the best between Cremona and Mantua – are worth a visit. The latter is usually locked, but the local priest will have the key. It is filled with huge, ornate family tombs, some in the form of temples, others devised as grottoes, and all tributes to an extraordinarily powerful faith.

About half-way to Mantua the road crosses the Oglio, a fine, sedate river which flows into the Po at Scorzarolo and marks the border of the province of Mantua. Its banks, like those of the Po further south, are thickly planted with poplars, refreshingly green even at the height of summer and casting a welcome shade.

Mantua stands on the Mincio where the river has widened into a large area of marsh and four lakes – Superiore, Mezzo, Inferiore and Paiolo – which enclose the city on all sides. The northern tip of Mantua is also separated from the main body of the town by the Rio Sottoriva, which links lakes Superiore and Inferiore and in places resembles a Venetian canal. This waterway can be compared with the real thing by joining one of the two-day boat trips to Venice down the Po, into which the Mincio flows a dozen kilometres to the south. These begin in the small harbour, the Porto Catena, where the Sottoriva runs into Lake Inferiore. Like all towns close to a large expanse of water, Mantua benefits from reflection off the lakes, and as you approach it, especially on a bright day, the quality of the light subtly changes. But the water and swamps also bring disadvantages. In summer, the town becomes exceedingly humid and it is frequently foggy in winter. Even so, Mantua is a memorable place, rich in atmosphere and in monuments reflecting a sumptuous past under the Gonzagas.

It seems probable that there was an Etruscan settlement here in the seventh century BC, though some authorities consider the original foundation of the city was more recent, around 140 BC. According to legend, and as recorded by Dante in the *Inferno*, the Greek soothsayer Manto fled here from Thebes and founded the city with her son Ocnus. Whatever its origins, Mantua has undoubtedly had a complicated and at times violent history during the last two thousand years, and has been fought over and occupied by the Romans, Franks, Huns and Byzantines. In the Middle Ages, two families in particular contributed significantly to the city's development, the Bonacolsis and the Gonzagas.

With a population of around 60,000, Mantua is about three-quarters the size of Cremona, yet it appears bigger. It has few of the kind of really narrow streets that always add charm to a place and, because pedestrian areas are limited, cars are a particular menace, especially when driven over cobbles at high speed. Indeed there is a growing concern about this problem and about pollution, and a number of demonstrations have been held in recent years in an attempt to stimulate some action. Although industry here, which includes paper-making and chemical plants, is both considerable and varied, Mantua is not an industrial town. Nor does it rank as a major port, despite its inevitable reliance on water. But while the lakes do not feature amongst Italy's greatest, they are an unexpected attraction. They are calm, even sluggish, for most of the time, with gently sloping banks thick with rushes and wild flowers. The best time to enjoy them is in April or May when the weather is pleasantly warm, or in September, when a visit can be combined with a trip to the opera in Verona only 30 kilometres away. Even early in March the sun can be quite strong here, though local children are still sent off to school wearing ski-jackets, sweaters and gloves.

Mantua's real claim to international fame is its historic buildings. Certainly no other town in Lombardy can challenge the architectural wealth of its north-east corner, which is dominated by the forbidding brick façade of the moated Castello San Giorgio with its towers overlooking the lake. Immediately to the south is the Palazzo Ducale and Piazza Sordello. On Saturdays the piazza is covered with stalls, part of a market for all kinds of produce and manufactured goods stretching south through the town to the

Soaring poplars provide welcome breaks in the vast vistas of the Po valley.

The Rio Sottoriva, the canal which cuts off the
northern tip of Mantua, offers a foretaste of Venice.

Sottoriva. The biggest open market in northern Italy, it
is the scene of some very substantial business deals.

The *palazzo*, where the Corte Vecchio dates from
1290, was begun in the thirteenth century by the
Bonacolsis. Thereafter the Gonzagas added to it over
four centuries until it became the biggest of its kind in
Europe, with over 500 rooms and a maze of corridors,
beautifully arcaded courtyards, and squares with
gardens on different levels. The interior, decorated
with great richness throughout, includes some striking
features. There is the spiral staircase big enough for
horses to be taken up and down, with brick steps to
ensure they would not slip. There are the apartments
for the court dwarfs, the Casetta dei Nani, with low

ceilings and shallow stairs specially designed for them. One room has its ceiling decorated with a labyrinth, the Gonzaga emblem, with the motto of Vincenzo I inscribed in the different sections: '*Forse cheno, forse chesi*' ('Perhaps no, perhaps yes'). The intricate design must have given many a visitor a painful neck as they tried to trace the way to the centre.

The art collection housed here is outstanding. Particularly vivid are the battle scenes from the Arthurian legends in the fifteenth-century frescoes by the Veronese artist Antonio Pisanello, only discovered in 1969 during restoration work. A painting of another battle, by Domenico Morone, dating from 1494, depicts the expulsion of the Bonacolsi family. Almost as impressive as Pisanello's work are the tapestries from Brussels by Dieter van Aelst depicting scenes from the New Testament; they are based on drawings by Raphael, commissioned by Pope Leo X in 1514 for the Sistine Chapel. But these – all in the first two suites of rooms you see – are overshadowed by the frescoes in the square Camera degli Sposi painted between 1465 and 1474 by Andrea Mantegna. Here there are portraits of the Gonzagas at the time of Lodovico. Of them all, the best-known is the fresco depicting the meeting between Lodovico and his son Francesco, recently made a cardinal, who is surrounded by the Gonzaga children; their linked hands symbolize family unity and continuity. The group is set against an idealized landscape which includes the Coliseum in Rome. The work is best known for Mantegna's attempt to create perspective, but the delicacy of the colours and the distant, unworldly quality in the eyes of humans and animals alike are just as striking. About a third of the way down the design on the false pillar to the right of the main door into this room is a cleverly hidden self-portrait by Mantegna. Once you notice it, you have the impression that your response to the frescoes is being carefully assessed.

Across Piazza Sordello is the thirteenth-century cathedral of San Pietro, which was restored three hundred years later by Giulio Romano. In the mid eighteenth century a pretentious façade was added, but the interior recalls the simplicity of early Christian churches. The nave is above ground-level and is flanked by aisles which in turn open on to chapels, creating a sense of great space. Particularly notable and in keeping with San Pietro's general atmosphere is a plain fifth-century sarcophagus in the first chapel on the south side. Next to the cathedral is Palazzo Vescovile, now the home of an expensive restaurant, and from here a series of interlinked narrow streets leads north to Piazza Virgiliana – in fact a park – shaded with planes, acacias, firs and poplars and with the poet's statue in gleaming white marble. A zigzag route south from here by way of Via Virgilio, Via Cavour and Vicolo Fieno brings you to Piazza Matilde di Canossa. This is not on any recognized tourist beat, but the splendid seventeenth-century Palazzo Canossa in the piazza, now the offices of the local Jehovah's Witnesses, has an impressive monumental staircase guarded by two marble dogs and adorned by classical statues carrying torches. Also, the neighbouring Caffe Canossa is an excellent place to sit, read the papers, or watch the Mantuans going about their business.

From Piazza Sordello you can also go south-west by way of Via Broletto to see the architectural wealth of Piazza delle Erbe. In the south-eastern corner is the beautiful eleventh-century brick rotunda of San Lorenzo, with a stairway cut inside the walls giving access to the ladies' gallery. An arcaded fifteenth-century house diagonally opposite belonged to a wealthy merchant, Giovanni da Concorezzo, who decorated its façade with intricate Venetian and oriental designs in terracotta. Here, too, is the fifteenth-century basilica church of San Andrea, notable for its huge barrel roof and the absence of pillars separating the nave from the side aisles; as in San Pietro, this creates a sense of enormous space. The sides of the church are lined with richly ornate chapels and an eighteenth-century cupola over the crossing is decorated with a painting of the Adoration of God by the Seven Stages of Creation. The chapel where Mantegna is buried, the first on the left, contains a rather sour-faced bust of the artist, which some authorities say is his own work! In the crypt are two vessels which supposedly contain samples of Christ's blood, said to have been brought to

Left One of the two medallions decorating the west façade of the cathedral of San Pietro, Mantua.

Above The eighteenth-century façade of the cathedral contrasts strongly with the medieval austerity of Piazza Sordello which it fronts.

Above A fragment of the beautifully decorated ceiling of the entrance to the cathedral in Mantua.

Right This delicate stonework can be seen in Piazza delle Erbe in Mantua, where it adorns a fifteenth-century house originally built for a Milan merchant called Boniforte.

The rotunda of San Lorenzo, Mantua.

Mantua and buried by Longino, the soldier who pierced Christ's side, was converted to Christianity and fled to Italy. On Good Friday the vessels are carried with due ceremony in procession through the town.

Just east of Piazza delle Erbe is the eighteenth-century Teatro Scientifico, designed by Antonio Bibiena in 1769; the opening concert was given in 1770 by a thirteen-year-old prodigy called Mozart. The theatre is regularly used and its sumptuous interior with three tiers of boxes is best admired when packed with elegant Mantuans gathered for a performance.

Like Cremona, Mantua has a wealth of *palazzi*; some, such as the early seventeenth-century Palazzo Gonzaga di Vescovato in Via Carlo Pana which houses the law courts, are public institutions, others privately owned. Two, in particular, are justifiably major attractions: the Palazzo del Te to the south, next to the

race course, and the Palazzo d'Arco near the railway station.

The Palazzo del Te, designed in the sixteenth century by Giulio Romano for Federico Gonzaga, derives its name from the swampy island, Tejeto, on which it was built and which was the site of a stud farm. From the outside it is somewhat austere, but the inner courtyard planted with lawns and parterres is more intimate. Old prints and pictures show there to have been a maze of box hedges here, another reminder of the Gonzaga emblem. Inside the palace many of the rooms are painted with allegorical figures and with riotous, fantastic scenes. Visit in particular the Sala di Psiche, once a dining-room, or the Sala dei Giganti. The former contains frescoes depicting muscular, lascivious satyrs being fed fruit by scantily dressed, voluptuous ladies, scenes which are said to reflect the extravagant, liberal life-style of the first owner. The latter tells the story of the vengeance of Jupiter on the giants who dared to conspire against him. The Sala dei Cavalli where arriving guests would have been received, with its life-size models of horses, or the Camera degli Stucchi with its two-tiered frieze depicting Roman military campaigns, are more sober, though equally sumptuous. In the north-west corner of the garden is the Casino della Grotta, once a bathing-place and even today retaining an air of intimacy and pleasure.

Unfortunately, the *palazzo* has been unfurnished for several years, and while this allows you to appreciate the decoration to the full, the effect is rather sterile. Happily this is not the case in the eighteenth-century Palazzo d'Arco, where period furniture is set off by some splendid oak and walnut floors. Worth attention, too, are the many fine paintings, notably one in Room XI showing St Thomas touching Christ's wound on the *left* side of his body. Various archaeological remains (including some fine Roman jars), and a painting of the genealogical tree of the Agnelli family are displayed in a small outbuilding in the garden. On the first floor is a fascinating room decorated with

In Piazza delle Erbe, Mantua.

allegories based on the signs of the Zodiac, where I could happily have spent at least an hour. Unfortunately this was not possible, as the guide taking me round would allow no one to linger. Conducted tours in Mantua generally are very variable. Those organized by the tourist office in Piazza delle Erbe are thorough; those conducted by people working in individual buildings are not, and can amount to a caricature of what such a tour should be. Attempts have been made to improve matters, but interests are strongly entrenched and the unions representing the two groups are locked in disagreement.

Other striking buildings not to be missed include the fifteenth-century church of San Sebastiano in Via Acerbi and, just opposite, the house of the painter Mantegna, who was induced to settle in Mantua by Lodovico Gonzaga. San Sebastiano was designed on a grand scale by Leon Battista Alberti, but he died before it could be finished. Construction was continued by the much less distinguished Antonio Abaco and the result is a curious mixture. Beneath the church is a massive crypt roofed by five barrel vaults which rise above ground-level. Access to the church today is up two flights of steps at the front, but these were not added until 1925. Before that it was through a loggia on the north side, but this too is clearly of a much later date than the original church. Just how people got in 500 years ago remains a mystery. By comparison, Mantegna's house, now appropriately an art school, is simple. It is built in the form of a cube with a round inner courtyard, the base of a cylinder which rises through the building and was once covered by a dome. A date carved in one of the bricks indicates that construction began in 1476, though progress must have been remarkably slow, for Mantegna only seems to have moved here in 1494. Painstaking restoration and the addition of some large windows have accentuated the clean geometric lines and allowed even more light to flood into the building for the benefit of

Mantegna's present-day disciples.

A word, too, should be said about food in Mantua. Even more than in the rest of Lombardy, eating here is a social as well as a gastronomic ritual. Food tends to be basic, perhaps reflecting the region's close connection with the soil. Pasta dishes and soups are much in evidence, among them *agnoli* or *tortelli di zucca*, small pasta pouches stuffed with meat or pumpkin, and *broda*, a soup made from beef, garlic, chicken, celery, onion and carrot, all wonderfully sustaining on a cold winter's day. Duck (*cappone alla Gonzaga*) is a local speciality, but try the more ordinary *stracotto*, a filling dish of beef marinated and stewed in wine. This is usually served with *polenta*, which is often flavoured with garlic or toasted in slabs. And there is always donkey. Fish of many varieties is plentiful and the *torta sbrisolana* made from yellow flour, almonds, lard and eggs has to be sampled. All can be very satisfactorily washed down with a jug of the most ordinary Lambrusco, which should not be too warm. In Via Trieste just off the eastern end of the Sottoriva is the Antica Osteria ai Ranari, where all these dishes can be tried in a noisy, friendly atmosphere. And after sampling such delights, nothing is more pleasant than walking the length of the canal, particularly on an early summer evening when the window-boxes are bright with flowers and the air is fresh.

From Mantua the south-eastern and furthermost part of Lombardy is easily explored in a day. The countryside is much the same as it is east of Cremona, with vast tracts of fertile land carefully prepared in March for abundant crops of cereals, rice, vegetables and fruit, especially melons. Despite the long hours of sunlight and high humidity, kilometres of seed drills are covered with plastic stretched over hoops to hasten growth. Some of these tunnels even have smaller, similarly constructed tubes inside and lie across the fields with their end flaps open like rows of great gaping silver slugs. There are also long trellises of fruit trees and again the odd row of tall vines. It was in this area that I once stopped to talk to two elderly Italians busily engaged in pruning the vines, who I thought might be able to tell me about them. Unfortunately, I

Arcaded stairs and greenery by the law courts in Mantua.

could make no more of their dialect than they could of my Italian; we parted on the best of terms, but with my ignorance intact.

The water essential for this agricultural activity comes from the Po, and from the Secchia which joins it at Mirasole, with a system of deep irrigation canals leading it to the fields. Sand and gravel workings exist in several places and at Ostiglia, for centuries an important crossing-point on the Po, there is a thermo-electric power station whose cooling towers dominate the whole area. Despite its twentieth-century appearance, however, Ostiglia is ancient, recorded in history since 130 BC and probably very much older. Pieces of Etruscan sculpture and pottery have been found here and are now on display in the Palazzo Ducale in Mantua, but the local council has kept a fine ancient sarcophagus which sits proudly in the stair-well of the municipal offices.

Between Ostiglia and Mantua is San Benedetto Po, a rapidly expanding agricultural centre where, on the first Sunday of October, the traditional local dish of duck (*al nedar*) is offered to all who crowd into the main square. But the principal reason for coming here is to see the Benedictine monastery and basilica church, the Abbazia di Polirone, built on land given to the monks by Tebaldo di Canossa. Parts of the former, which dates from 1007, are currently being restored and are closed, but there is still much to see. There are the two cloisters, the second of which, the Chiostri di San Benedetto, was rebuilt in the sixteenth century. The monastery's hospital is still in a semi-ruined state, but the refectory has been restored and gives some idea of the spartan splendour that the monks enjoyed. The basilica church, dominating Piazza Teofilo Folengo, was built in the late sixteenth century but stands on foundations certainly 400 years older. It has a magnificent roof inset with geometric shapes and there is a series of paintings above the five arches along each side of the nave depicting scenes from both Old and New Testaments. In the south-eastern entrance to the apse is

the alabaster tomb of Mathilda of Canossa (who gave money to the monastery), with four red marble lions grandly supporting the chest.

Directly east, 10 kilometres across the Secchia, is the village of Quingentole, reached by a minor road which passes several walled cemeteries with a characteristic range of modern monumental tombs. Quingentole is remarkable for its enormous square (the work of the Gonzaga family), with arcading to the north, south and east, and for the equally imposing eighteenth-century church of San Lorenzo. Despite the fine pair of marble lions guarding its west façade, this is in poor condition, with peeling plaster and crumbling masonry, but the sheer scale of the centre of this small – if now growing – village is impressive. A tiny barber's shop with a tiled front in the south-east corner of the square has what must be a rare collection of hairdressing posters from the 1950s.

Felonica, the most eastern village of Lombardy and famous nation-wide for its onions, is now less than half an hour away. The road to it continues along the south bank of the Po through Revere, where there is a severe, military-looking, fifteenth-century house with squat, roofed turrets built for the Gonzagas by Luca Fancelli. Today it contains the local municipal offices.

Going north, Mantua can easily be avoided by continuing on the S482 from Ostiglia through Frassino and bypassing the city to the east. The S236 to Goito runs north-west, past fields of canes cultivated for basket-making and furniture, and pig farms rearing animals destined to end up as salami and ham. At Goito, about 16 kilometres from Mantua, marked by extensive gravel workings on the Mincio, fork right, and due north, to Volta. This whole area, where the land begins to rise away from the vast plains of the Po and Mincio valleys, was once covered by an immense forest extending north to the edge of Lake Garda. Now arable land dominates, with patches of vineyards on the stony higher ground. The air is fresher here and Volta is an ideal place for curing (and sampling) the hams brought up from the plain.

Instead of heading directly north to Lake Garda, only 20 kilometres away, make a detour to take in

Haymaking and poplars in the Po valley.

Left There is a strong hint of the pagan in this figure at San Benedetto Po.

Right Decorated with medals, a stern Napoleon III reflects on his victory at Solferino in 1859 in the Franco-Austrian war.

Cavriana and Solferino. As you top the rise out of Volta, the mountains of the Veneto and the eastern ranges of Brescia province dominate the view, in places reaching to over 3000 metres. To the left, the busy, delightful hill village of Cavriana is entered through the one surviving fourteenth-century gate. Here there is a rather magnificent eighteenth-century church and the remains of two castles from the twelfth and fourteenth centuries. People in the tiny post-office were much amused when I requested stamps for cards to Australia and the United States, yet the village's past is cosmopolitan enough. The fifteenth-century Villa Mirra-Siliprandi has provided hospitality for Napoleon III, Victor Emanuele II and Charles de Gaulle.

The neighbouring village of Solferino, only 4 kilometres away, is much better known. This was the site of the great Risorgimento victory of 24 June 1859 over the Austrians, in a terrible battle which resulted in 15,000 dead. In 1870 it was decided to turn the tower of San Pietro, a baroque church standing on a hillock just outside the village, into a memorial and ossuary; it is said that nearly 1500 skulls and thousands of bones were gathered together and stored here. Solferino is also celebrated as the place where the idea for the Red Cross organization was conceived by a young Swiss banker, Henri Dunant. He had been in the area at the time of the battle and, with the help of some women from the nearby village of Castiglione, had organized primitive medical care. The experience so moved him that he wrote a book about it which became a bestseller. Within five years his idea that the sick and wounded in battle should be given immediate neutral status, as should those caring for them, was developed formally into the Red Cross. Dunant was awarded the Nobel Prize in 1901.

From Solferino, instead of going on to the larger community of Castiglione, cut up north-east through Pozzolengo and San Martino della Battaglia. Pozzolengo is the best of the fortified hilltop villages to be found in this area, all of which are built at heights of between 100 and 150 metres and are very reminiscent of the *villages perchés* in the south of France. Its walls are still largely intact, the round, roofed 'pepper-pot'

corner towers giving it a distinctive silhouette. San Martino a little further on boasts a 75-metre castellated tower built of pale brick dressed with darker stone. There are splendid views from the top across the very land which witnessed the defeat of the Austrians, and you can enter the heart of this country by picking out a route north to Desenzano and the lake using dirt roads only for much of the way.

After communities where the inhabitants are so clearly concerned mainly with the land and, from the reaction of the people in Cavriana's post-office, with their own immediate world, arrival in Desenzano is a shock. The road along the southern edge of Lake Garda to the Sirmione peninsula enters a region in which farm implements, sheds, ploughed fields and crops are replaced by fast-food restaurants, surfboard shops, and a multitude of flats, hotels, lidos, marinas and discotheques. This is an area to be avoided in high summer, when the local population is more than trebled by an influx of holiday-makers. Ideally, Sirmione should be visited in April and May, or September and October, when tourists are few, the weather is exceptionally agreeable and, if you go in spring, the flowers are at their most attractive. Olives, cypresses, lotuses, magnolias, palms, and other exotic trees and flowers give the impression that you are on the shores of the Mediterranean.

A winding road from Colombare leads to Sirmione at the end of a rocky peninsula which extends 3 kilometres into the lake, the last stretch of the route being lined with plane trees. All visitors are obliged to park their cars outside the village unless a booking has been confirmed with the tourist office and a permit obtained allowing you to drive into Sirmione and negotiate its narrow streets and one-way system. Apart from its natural beauty, Sirmione offers lovers of classical antiquity the splendidly preserved ruins of the Grotte di Catullo, the villa built by the family of the Roman poet Catullus, born in Verona around 84 BC and known in particular for his passionate addresses to a

Sirmione: all but the coconuts are grown locally.

married woman called Lesbia. The Grotte lies in an olive grove amidst clumps of shoulder-high rosemary at the very tip of the peninsula, poised 100 metres over the lake with magnificent views on both sides. Even today the ruins give a good idea of how palatial the villa must have been. Colonnades, rooms, doorways and stairways made of flint and brick create a harmonious whole. Particularly fine, in my opinion, is the row of eight linked arches lining what was clearly once a principal thoroughfare on the west side of the villa. It requires little imagination to picture toga-clad people elegantly going about their daily business here.

The setting is superb. Sometimes, in the late afternoon, the snow on the surrounding mountains is turned pink by the setting sun and the end of the lake 50 kilometres away at Riva can disappear mysteriously into the mist. No wonder Catullus could talk of Sirmione as the 'jewel of islands and peninsulas', even though he preferred the bustle and urbanity of Rome and only occasionally stayed here himself.

From the Grotte, the road climbs to the high point of Sirmione and the delightfully simple church of San Pietro, built in the eleventh century on the site of a church 300 years older. There are a number of frescoes, that of Christ in Majesty behind the plain block of rock which forms the altar almost certainly dating from the thirteenth century and striking in its colour and the boldness of the human representation of Christ. Sadly, however, the walls – and even the frescoes – have been despoiled by graffiti. A large bell and artillery gun outside commemorate those who lost their lives during World War II.

Whichever road you take from San Pietro instantly plunges you into the late twentieth century. To the west you pass a number of huge, modern, luxurious houses in Via San Pietro or Via Faustina owned by wealthy *milanesi*, their gardens dotted with reproductions of classical statues. Understandably enough, they are surrounded by tall fences and thick hedges studded with notices about fierce dogs. Slightly inland lies the villa that once belonged to Maria Callas. To the east a path cuts down to the lido, where the pedalos lie stacked in winter waiting for the summer invasion and

where the sunbeds are already prepared by May. Beyond the nearby Villa Cortine hotel, with classical statues, a folly and a nineteenth-century model of an ancient temple in its landscaped, terraced gardens, the medieval village begins.

Despite much modernization, the streets and houses clustered around the fifteenth-century church of San Maggiore have retained their medieval charm. A fresco in the church itself is one of the best illustrations I have seen of the paradox of bliss achieved through suffering that is so central to Christianity. St Sebastian gazes heavenwards, his face serene, his body cruelly pierced by no fewer than seventeen arrows.... The narrow streets and alleyways round about house many of Sirmione's 5000 inhabitants, all but a few of whom live off tourism; in the summer the population regularly doubles. There can be few places with such a high incidence of ice-cream parlours, restaurants and souvenir shops. It is wise to come here with a pack of credit cards!

Surprisingly, Sirmione is a spa. On the western side of the village and surrounded by impeccable gardens is a thermal centre for the treatment of deafness and bronchial problems where 'aesthetic medicine' is also practised. The water comes from a spring known as La Boiola in the bed of the lake a little to the east of the peninsula and is at a constant temperature of $32°-34°C$. Quite different in character is the Rocca Scaligera, the thirteenth-century fortress which guards the narrow strip of land leading to Sirmione and also overlooks the fortified harbour once used by the Lake Garda fleet. The castle houses some Roman and medieval remains, but it is especially interesting for the sense of almost total impregnability once you are inside, and the views over the lake are stunning. As you leave Sirmione, it is easy to imagine the drawbridge being pulled up behind you.

As around Mantua, the countryside between here and Brescia is predominantly agricultural, dotted with

The forbidding fortifications protecting the landward approaches to Sirmione on Lake Garda.

Soncino's Sforza castle is one of the best preserved in Lombardy.

large farmsteads and silos which suggest considerable wealth. And yet, though similar, it is not quite the same. Fields are smaller and there are more rows of trees – brutally pruned in late winter – acting as wind-breaks.

Having returned along the peninsula to Desenzano, make for Lonato. Park at the main gate of the cemetery and walk up to the imposing Casa del Podesta, a reconstruction of the original fourteenth-century castle which today houses an important library with nearly a thousand manuscripts. It is open to the public but it hardly feels like a place of study, its sheer bulk and position making its former military role impossible to forget.

The agricultural plain to the west holds little of particular interest. Castiglione, a moderate-sized place, does have some interesting buildings, in particular the fifteenth-century Collegiata with some fine frescoes illustrating the lives of Mary, St Lawrence and St Stephen, but this town and Montichiari (a sprawling centre with a lot of new – and very English – residential development), Ghedi and Manerbio can be passed with scarcely a glance. Take the first opportunity to wander off the main road – once again often only possible by dirt tracks – to Orzinuovi, where the gatehouse and huge square are a reminder of medieval power and splendour. Soncino, 4 kilometres away, is a small, walled town with its fifteenth-century Sforza castle facing boldly south-west. Although in generally good condition, the fortress is being completely restored. It is built around two interconnecting court-yards with corner towers linked by long covered galleries on the first floor and, despite its great age, is remarkably draught-free. Originally moated, it was approached across the drawbridge on the north-eastern side.

Soncino, which has been here since the fourth century, has other delights too. The village's principal church, the fifteenth-century Santa Maria Assunta, has a magnificent altar and a blue timber roof pat-terned with stars. Around the choir and altar marble predominates, but towards the west end the central aisle is flanked by brick pillars with frescoes above the arches. A small altar on the north wall holds a relic of St Joseph. The second church, Santa Maria delle Grazie (1492–1528), just a few hundred metres to the south-west of Soncino, has an extraordinarily rich interior decorated with multi-coloured terracotta and frescoes by Giulio Campi and a family of local sixteenth-century artists – Allegrino, Ermete and Francesco Scanzi.

Before leaving the village, see the restored medieval house in Via IV Novembre and the arcaded brick galleries of no. 8 in Via de Baris. In this same area, in Via della Orfanella, is the Mulino di Borgo San Angelo, a water-mill which looks as though it is several hundred years old and still retains its wheel. Every-where in Soncino there is an air of pride and activity, neatly summarized by a series of modern terracotta plaques in Via Orefici depicting the months of the year, seasonal activities and children's games. Tourists are attracted here and in the summer both they and local people take advantage of the nearby Oglio river, where shallow pools are ideal for bathing and banks of shingle for sitting, talking, and having picnics. There are fishing competitions, events based on local folklore in September and in November the traditional raft-race, the *Sagra del Radicchio*, for which the teams dress in local costume. Controlling the rafts is no mean feat as the river has already begun to swell considerably with autumn rain.

From Soncino to Crema takes about fifteen minutes and as you approach the town the atmosphere changes quite abruptly. Although Crema has no more than 50,000 inhabitants, it has all the characteristics of a much larger place, with industrial outskirts where foodstuff and pharmaceutical factories, garages and engineering works are prominent. Just as Lodi her-alded the countryside of the Po valley, so Crema heralds Milan.

Yet it is more than an adjunct or dormitory of the city to the west, and the modern face of Crema hides an ancient town entered by the medieval Porta Ombriano. There was a settlement here well before the Roman occupation and maps and prints in the town's museum indicate that the layout of the oldest part of the town has hardly changed for at least five centuries. The cathedral, said to be one of the finest churches in the Lombard romanesque style, dominates the arcaded central square, flanked by the elegant Palazzo del Comune (1525), still used as municipal offices, and the arcaded Palazzo Pretorio (1552–5), with its brick tower. In the summer, with café tables spreading across it, the square is a busy, colourful place, and even in winter the arcades make it welcoming.

Despite the cathedral's reputation, its west front looks to me too large, as though added at the last moment. This impression is created, I think, by the fact the brick façade rises *above* the roofs of the side aisles, with two beautifully decorated pierced openings like glassless windows level with the central rose window. The sense of height this composition creates is in-creased by the frieze of white pillars crowning the gabled front and by the three turrets with conical spires which rise above it. The six-stage campanile and clock tower at the eastern end of the church, also constructed in brick, supports an elaborate octagonal belfry with multiple open arcades and a spire matching those on the west front.

By comparison, the interior is less impressive. The

Left Two of a series of terracotta plaques in Soncino illustrating the seasons and the villagers' traditional activities.

Right *Cascina* and campanile just north of Crema. The shabby exteriors of these buildings often hide considerable wealth.

altar, organ and glass are all modern, but there are the remains of some frescoes and a delightful sixteenth-century Virgin and Child towards the east end. A harrowing modern mural of the Descent from the Cross can be seen in the vestry, and there is a moving and much admired fourth-century wooden crucifix at the end of the north aisle.

Not far from the cathedral square is the curious, almost cylindrical, renaissance Santa Maria della Croce of 1490–1500, at the end of Viale della Stazione, and also the baroque San Giacomo Maggiore, in Via Matteotti, decorated throughout with frescoes of the life of John the Baptist by the seventeenth-century local artist, Gian Barbelli. San Domenico in Viale della Stazione has become a gymnasium, and Crema's library and museum is housed in what was the convent of San Agostino, in Via Dante. The refectory of this former Augustinian monastery has been transformed into a lecture hall, and visitors can wander in the cloisters. The museum itself is not nearly as well frequented as it deserves. A collection of frescoes and paintings of all kinds and periods, archaeological discoveries, prints, maps and a room devoted to the period of Garibaldi occupy the first floor. More intriguing, however, is the room on the floor below, where fourteen medieval paintings depict people from all ranks of society – pope, king and pauper – in their appropriate robes –

but as skeletons. A macabre reminder indeed of one's mortality.

In addition, Crema has a number of *palazzi* in various states of repair, of which the part-ruined early eighteenth-century Palazzo Terni with classical figures adorning the front wall is particularly striking. But compared, for example, with Cremona, there seems little real concern for monuments from the past. Look into the courtyard of no. 7 in Via Ponte Furio on the west side of town. Here a collection of serviceable pieces of masonry spanning a period of at least 400 years is thrown together like a vast historic rubbish dump.

A few kilometres outside Crema on the main S415 to Milan turn right to Palazzo Pignano and Pandino. The origins of the former are still a subject of considerable debate, but from the mosaics and foundations which have been uncovered it is now certain that there was an important Roman settlement here, and the eleventh-century church of Pieve di San Martino is on the site of one that was 500 years older.

The castle at Pandino, erected by the Viscontis, is young in comparison, dating only from the late fourteenth century. Centuries later it became a farm, but now houses the local municipal offices and has been lavishly restored. The main gate, the galleries on the first floor and the frescoes – particularly those on the vaulting of the arcades around the central courtyard – are all impressive and modern office efficiency has not been allowed to erase a sense of the past. Employees here will show you what has been achieved with some pride. As a final reminder of the medieval splendour of Lombardy's great plain, the Castello Visconti at Pandino is difficult to better.

The carefully restored Visconti castle of Pandino, now the local municipal offices.

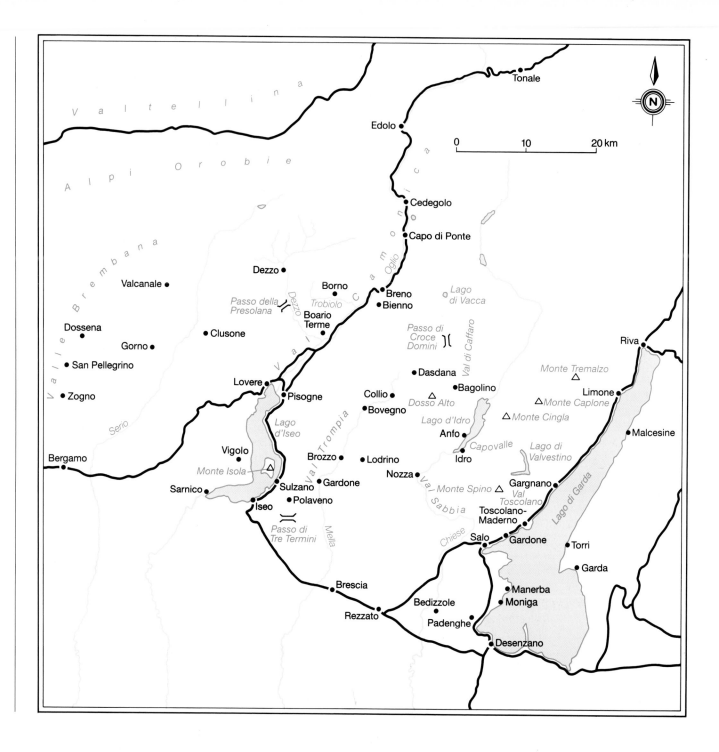

3
The Heartland: Lakes Garda and Iseo

Brescia – Lake Garda – Salo – Gardone – Limone – Lake Idro
– Bagolino – Breno – Val Camonica – Lake Iseo – Monte Isola
– Lovere – Clusone – San Pellegrino – Bergamo

The largely mountainous provinces of Bergamo and Brescia cover the area east of Milan from the Valtellina to the western shore of Lake Garda. The two capital cities sit on the southern edges of their provinces and both can be reached from Milan in an hour or so by road or rail. Brescia, Lombardy's second largest city, is equally easily reached from Mantua. The whole area is crossed south to north by a series of valleys, such as the Brembana or the Camonica, which lead north to the Orobie Alps. The Lago d'Iseo, Italy's fourth biggest lake, lies in the centre of the region and a number of others, some no more than large ponds, are hidden away in tiny, sheltered valleys.

The road from Milan to Brescia crosses the fertile plain watered by the Adda and Serio, an intensively cultivated area scattered with imposing and self-evidently wealthy, modernized *cascini*. Ditches cleared by early spring to cope with the overflow from streams and rivers swollen by melting snow form a watery grid, dead weeds hanging on the trees and bushes along their banks like grey shrouds.

To the north, the hills push down towards the road and it is soon apparent that Brescia has had little choice but to develop principally towards the south. As a result, approached from this direction, the centre of the old city seems a long time in coming, an impression that is made worse if you arrive by car and become a helpless victim of the one-way system. Rather than plunging into the centre of the town, however, start by visiting the castle overlooking Brescia from the north where the panorama over the city gives a bird's-eye view of its layout and development. What is most striking – and will be confirmed at a lower level – is the impression of space at the very heart of the town, created by a series of virtually interconnecting *piazzi*. You can also see how tightly packed the houses are, especially in what were – and in a way still are – the more working-class areas to the west.

The position of the castle is a reminder of the settlement of Brixia, as Brescia was originally called, a name based, according to tradition, on the Ligurian word *brik*, meaning 'hill'. In the first century BC the Romans established an important camp on this site and there are traces of a fifth-century church (San Stefano) and of an archway from the same period. The castle seen today was largely built in the fourteenth century by the Visconti family, with the round Mirabella tower dating from a hundred years before. These buildings now house a military museum, and a good one too for those who find the history of armaments interesting, and the Cidnea observatory. Brescia's zoo is laid out in the gardens.

Down the hill in Brescia itself, begin to explore from the centre. Three of the most important buildings, the two cathedrals and the *broletto*, stand side by side in Piazza del Duomo. The old cathedral, or Rotonda, is stunningly beautiful in its simplicity and compares well with the one in Mantua. As its name suggests, it is round, or drum-shaped, with a cylindrical tower supported by eight sturdy columns. In the late fifteenth century, a raised choir was added. The building is now half-buried, though on completion in the eleventh century it was entered at a lower level. Beneath the apse (where the plaster is in poor condition) is the crypt of St Filastrio, one of the first to bring Christianity to this part of Lombardy. On the north side of the high altar are the treasures of the Holy Cross (*Santissimi Croci*), including pieces of wood and a thorn from Christ's crown, all of which are shown to the faithful on the last Friday of March.

While it is known as 'new', the more recent cathedral was in fact begun in 1604, though it was not completed until two centuries later, in 1825, when the central dome was finally added. The Duomo Nuovo stands on the site of the former basilica of San Pietro, which had to be demolished in 1595, so a notice informs us, 'because of decrepitude'! It is a massive building, cold in temperature and, by comparison with its neighbour, in spirit as well. Even the curious bust of Cardinal Querini with its somewhat condescending expression does little to encourage the faithful as they arrive for worship.

The rectangular *broletto*, dating from the eleventh century, is built round a courtyard. The principal tower, the Torre del Popolo, dominates the whole complex and is held by many to be the best in Lombardy. On the first floor of the west façade of the courtyard is a fine brick window which has somehow escaped a series of restorations over the centuries. Before it moved to the Loggia (see below), Brescia's council used to meet in the *broletto* and one of the balconies from which proclamations would be made can be seen in the inner courtyard. The *broletto* still houses offices, but for all the affection in which it appears to be held by local people it is in need of attention. Cardinal Querini, who greets visitors to the new cathedral, founded the Biblioteca Queriniana in Via Mazzini, just to the east of the cathedral square, in the seventeenth century. This library contains one of the most important collections of rare books and manuscripts in northern Italy, including a very handsome fourteenth-century English Psalter. But it is also the municipal library, much used by students and the general public. The seemingly endless reading-rooms have painted ceilings and are lined with leather-bound volumes, often locked away behind protective grilles. A garden in the central courtyard is partly, and rather delightfully, planted with vegetables, and readers sit here in the summer in the shade of fruit trees and trained climbing plants.

From Piazza del Duomo it is only two or three minutes' walk to the adjoining squares, the Piazzi Vittoria, Loggia and Mercato. Of these, the second contains the Loggia, the new (sixteenth-century) council building, designed by many hands but nevertheless remarkably uniform. An astrological clock in the same piazza, modelled on the one in St Mark's Square in Venice, is topped by two figures who strike the hours. And across the corner of the square is the handsome Palazzo del Monte Nuova di Pietà, built just at the end of the sixteenth century and regularly used for exhibitions.

The rest of the old town is easily explored from this central area. To the east of the squares, along Via dei Musei behind the cathedrals, is the oldest, Roman section of Brescia. As the street name suggests, there is a wealth of material to be discovered here and it is advisable to buy a ticket which will give you access to all monuments and buildings, even though restoration work can result in any or several of them being closed. Major excavations were in fact begun in the spring of 1989, and are likely to continue for one or two more years at least. As a consequence, the church of San Salvatore is currently shut, which is a pity. The

---

Begun at the end of the fifteenth century, the loggia, like the cathedral, is referred to as 'new'.

Left **The strong-minded benefactor Cardinal Querini looks heavenwards for assistance in Brescia cathedral.**

Above **The astrological clock in Piazza del Loggia, Brescia, is modelled on the one in St Mark's Square in Venice.**

original church on this site, founded in 753 by Desiderius, duke of Lombardy, was rebuilt during the reign of Charlemagne at the beginning of the ninth century and substantially modified 500 years later. It has three interconnecting naves and on the northern side a staircase leads down to a minute crypt that is so densely packed with forty-two pillars that there is hardly room to turn round. In the main church are a number of important frescoes, dating from the ninth to the sixteenth century and depicting biblical scenes and the exploits of various saints. There is an especially good one of St George spearing his dragon, though the painting has been interestingly but regrettably defaced with names and initials inscribed over the last 400 years.

Also as a result of the excavations, much of the material in the Museo Cristiano (normally in the church of Santa Giulia) has been temporarily removed to the main art gallery in Via Marettok, named after Maretto da Brescia, the town's most famous painter, who lived and worked here in the sixteenth century. Here you can see some of the finest examples of early and medieval Christian art in Europe: the Lipsanoteca, an ivory reliquary from the fourth century (though largely reworked in 1928); the Croce di Desiderio, studded with semi-precious stones and so-called because it was said to have been presented by Desiderius, the eighth-century duke who founded San Salvatore; and fourteen other gold crosses 'recovered' from Lombardy tombs.

In addition to these buildings, you can visit the remains of the Roman Tempio Capitolino, built in AD 73 for the Emperor Vespasian. An entrance arch, colonnade, temple, theatre and forum are the main features of an impressively large site. A museum displays smaller, more intimate items – pieces of statuary, ceramics, glass, money and so on – from the Roman and other periods, the most notable exhibit being the elegant, bronze statue 2 metres tall known as the winged victory, the *Vittoria Alata*. There are also six gilded busts of Roman emperors and a small figure in bronze which is thought to represent the Gaulish chief Vercingetorix. (The collection owes much to the commendable foresight of Brescia's council in the late fifteenth century, which forbade the sale of antiques and treasures.)

Around this north-eastern corner of town, the narrow lanes have changed little over four or five centuries, but in comparison with the more working-class district to the west have become the focus for up-market jewellery, fashion and antique shops and smart apartments. One advantage of such developments is a concern for the buildings' fabric. On the corner of Vicoli Veronica, Gambara and Lungo, for example, a boutique trades from a beautifully maintained house with an exquisite inner courtyard and garden and false beam ends decorated with a series of marvellously expressive faces. And only 100 metres or so away a row of very full breasted, smiling maidens adorn the Palazzo Cigola in Piazza Tebaldo Brusato.

Shaded by chestnut trees, Piazza Tebaldo Brusato is a pleasant place to sit in summer, though it is not unusual to find tramps sleeping here, a reminder of another side to Brescia's character. This is particularly evident on the north-west side of town, where the streets are every bit as narrow, with many dead-ends and hidden squares, and full of tiny cafés and workshops concerned with furniture making and restoration. In general the streets are grubby and the buildings – externally at least – are less well tended, but there is the liveliness and buzz of a working community which is not found further east. And there are cats everywhere.

As in all Italian cities, there are a number of churches to explore in Brescia, some with adjoining cloisters and many full of fine works of art. Santissimo Corpo di Cristo, behind the Tempio Capitolino, is one that should not be missed. Consecrated in 1501, it has a marble main entrance, beautiful vaulting and frescoes dedicated to the disciples – Paolo da Caylina's depiction of the Virgin nursing the dead Christ is particularly harrowing. Since the 1950s this church has been owned by a missionary organization, but it is possible to visit the three cloisters on request, and this is also the case at the sixteenth-century San Giuseppe just north of Piazza Loggia. Near San Giuseppe is one of Brescia's – even Lombardy's – most curious churches, the twelfth-century San Faustino in Riposo, tucked in behind the Porta Brucia, one of the medieval gates. It is a minute, round church in an exquisite state of preservation, with a conical spire made of terracotta tiles and an astounding collection of sacred hearts, and it is always alive with worshippers and people who have simply arranged to meet here.

Finally, no visit to Brescia is complete without experiencing the Teatro Grande and its adjoining foyer, or *ridotto*. The classical auditorium, one of the finest in Italy, resembles a more intimate La Scala, the richly decorated ceiling, red furnishings and lavish gilding creating a sumptuous effect. The *ridotto*, a large rectangular room lined with three tiers of boxes on three sides, was built about fifty years later. It, too, is richly decorated and is used especially for chamber music. So frequent are performances – of concerts, opera, or plays – that both theatre and *ridotto* can be visited on most evenings throughout the year.

The quickest way to reach Lake Garda from Brescia is by the motorway. A more leisurely and enjoyable route to the western shore, however, is to leave the town by the S11 and, just beyond Rezzato, cross the Chiese river and follow the northern edge of the Brescia plain through Bedizzole. To the north, the hills are scarred with occasional quarries, but the land bordering the road is predominantly agricultural. North of Padenghe, bordering Garda's western shore, is the Valtenisi, known for its olives, while the region of Franciacorta north and west of here produces some fine wine, notably a few reds and a sparkling white, though the latter is not always made from grapes grown locally. A number of *cantine* – often quite splendid villas – publicize their produce and it is well worth stopping to sample what is on offer and appreciate how (justly) proud some of the wine-makers of this area are.

Garda is the largest of Italy's lakes, nearly 52 kilometres long and over 17 kilometres wide at its bulbous southern end. Together with Maggiore, it is scenically the most varied and dramatic as well. While the southern shore is bounded by the upper reaches of the great Lombardy plain, the eastern shore rises through wooded hills to the craggy peaks of the Monte Baldo range, several of which reach heights of over 2000 metres. To the north, a small alluvial plain is backed by mountains marking the border with Trentino, while to the west an attractive range of wooded hills and valleys, with occasional peaks over 1500 metres, stretches towards Val Sabbia and Lake Idro. Roads ring the water and a 144-kilometre round trip of the lake can be easily accomplished in a day.

The whole shore line from Desenzano to Salo is popular in summer, when the population increases alarmingly. Camp sites are numerous. During the high season the water temperature is around 24°C and, like the western shore of Lake Como, there is a distinctly Mediterranean feeling here, with luxuriant arrays of palms, mimosas and other exotic trees. An ideal time to visit is in April, when the weather is generally reliable, when villages are only just beginning to prepare for the summer and are not full to capacity, and when there is a freshness that has not yet been spoiled. On the other hand, I have known years when it has rained incessantly and heavily for three full days in April and blown a gale that has whipped the lake into something closely resembling a distinctly choppy sea. The winds here, the *sover* from the north and the *ora* from the south, are quite unpredictable, and Garda is immensely popular with sailing enthusiasts.

North along the lakeside, to the west of the S572, you come to Moniga, a tiny resort with houses actually built inside its medieval castle. Manerba, a few kilometres further on, is much bigger, with Roman tombstones in the fine twelfth-century church of Santa Maria. On the coast is a prominent headland known as the Rocca or, more evocatively, as Dante's profile, which has yielded evidence of man's presence since prehistoric times. From here a bay cuts sharply back into the hills to the west and the small town of Salo, long a trading point on the lake and still a busy port. It was at Salo that Mussolini set up the centre for his puppet fascist state in 1944, but today the town prefers to be remembered as the birthplace of Gasparo de Salo (1540–1609), thought by many to have invented the

Left By Riva on Lake garda, with the snow-capped mountains of Trentino beyond.

Above Salo on Lake Garda, birthplace of Gasparo de Salo, thought by many to have invented the violin.

violin, for its sprawling Saturday markets and for its sale of spirits, especially whiskey, of which, so it is said, any brand from anywhere in the world is on offer.

From Salo it is possible to follow the Chiese river along the Sabbia valley north to Lake Idro and beyond to the province of Trentino. Along Lake Garda itself, hills flecked with cypress trees now come down abruptly to the water, with only a narrow strip to carry the road along the remaining 50 kilometres to Riva. With spectacular sections where it passes through a series of tunnels and galleries cut out of the rock, this highway, the Gardesana Occidentale, has become one of the best known roads in Europe.

Two of the most popular resorts to have developed along this coast are Gardone and Toscolano-Maderno. The former is best known for its smart modern centre and, in the hills overlooking the town, for the Hruska botanical gardens, where more than 2000 species of plants, including many tropical exotics, have been planted since the late nineteenth century. Here, too, is the neo-classical Vittoriale, the last residence and burial place of Gabriele d'Annunzio, the poet, novelist and dramatist who died in 1938. Known not only as a writer but also as an extreme right-wing nationalist, d'Annunzio urged Italy to become involved in World War I. Such was his post-war popularity that Mussolini forced him to retire to this villa, which had originally belonged to a German family. Once installed, d'Annunzio decorated and furnished it in the most decadent, extravagant style. Preferring artificial light, he had many of the windows painted over; his study door is so low you have to bow as you enter; the master bedroom is draped in leopard skins and there is a small bed, designed like a coffin, in which he would lie when he communed with the world of the spirits. His body rests in a white marble mausoleum on a hill just above the villa, in a tomb raised on columns and surrounded by three rings of statues of Roman soldiers.

Much more modestly, Toscolano-Maderno is known for its long association with paper making and as the departure point for Torri on the opposite shore. Commercialism has left its indelible mark on both

resorts, and in my view it is better to go inland. Paths and unmade roads from either town follow valleys into the hills to reach the *rifugio* at the foot of the 1500-metre Monte Spino. Especially in summer, there is welcome relief here from the humidity that all too often characterizes the lakeside.

Between Maderno and the northern end of the lake, only Gargnano and Limone are of note, but even these relatively unspoilt villages have allowed some characterless building to take place in order to cater for an ever-growing tourist market. As its name suggests, Limone is famous for lemons, and these and other citrus fruits are grown in greenhouses and on south-facing terraces. Possibly because it is midway along this strip of coast, Gargnano remains a little under-developed, though there are signs that it too is beginning to realize the benefits to be had from tourism. A small pedestrian area flanked by a *gelateria* and a lakeside promenade are the first steps into late twentieth-century commercialism. But as yet the village retains much of its character. The harbour can only accommodate two dozen small boats at the most and many of the weathered houses facing the lake have not yet been subjected to fashionable smartening. One of the more splendid buildings is the Villa Feltinelli bordering the lake, now a centre providing courses for foreign students organized by the University of Milan. Out of season try the small café just behind the garage across the road from the villa. Here you will find photographs of the traditional boat races that are now staged as a tourist attraction, a wariness towards strangers and a primitive wood-fired brick stove whose single metal chimney warms the whole room. A kettle providing constant hot water sits on it day and night.

Like the other major lakes, Garda has an active boat service. Some of the ferries look distinctly past their best, but there are some smart hydrofoils which have been in operation for a few years and are impressive

The Grand Hotel and Mediterranean splendour at Gardone on Lake Garda.

both to watch and to travel on. Meals are served on some of the boats and a trip from, say, Maderno to Malcesine to the north on the opposite shore is a pleasant way to spend a summer's evening. But these boats move fast, and travelling on one of them will give you no more than a general impression of the lake. If time permits, take one of the less glamorous craft sailing slowly from port to port along sections of the coast. Round each headland and point something new is revealed, with glimpses of tiny beaches not visible from the road. Trellises of wood or concrete and wire create a curious effect. In summer these are covered with climbing plants or vines and provide welcome shade; in winter and spring when they are without their vegetation they look, especially from a distance, like a series of classical remains.

Between Garda and Lake Idro, the highest lake in Lombardy, lush valleys hiding the occasional hamlet wind into wooded hills. But except to the north, where the border with Trentino is marked by the peaks of Monti Cingla, Caplone and Tremalzo, the land rarely rises above 1500 metres. A good route from Gargnano leads by way of the Val Toscolano and the small, attractive lake of Valvestino to Capovalle, and beyond to Vantone on the eastern shore of Idro.

Although one of the region's principal lakes, Eridio, as Lake Idro was originally called, is probably the least attractive. Because of its colour — shades of green and pale purple are not unusual — local people like to think that it is rather like a Swiss lake. But that may be a defensive response. Certainly it is less dramatic than Garda or Iseo and bears no comparison with Como or Maggiore, though there are pleasing views to the north on fine days. The water is usually calm, trout fishing is good and the lake has become popular with tourists, in particular the Dutch, who colonize entire camp sites during the summer. The results of this popularity are inevitable, but the fun-fairs, fast-food establishments and camp sites around Crone, Idro or Anfo have the

Maderno on Lake Garda backed by a massive bank of cypress trees.

advantage that they draw attention away from the still attractive, older parts of some of the villages.

For reasons, so it is said, of local political rivalry, no road completely circles the lake, the north-eastern shore of which is the border with Trentino. From the north-western tip a minor road leads to Bagolino, twisting along the valley of the Caffaro river, across hillsides that are sometimes wooded. By the time the village is reached, you are 200 metres or so above the river, but the sound of the water is a constant presence. With a permanent population of about 5000, Bagolino is no lost village. It is busy all year round, and in recent years has expanded considerably. But unlike the lakeside villages below, it has retained its charm. Ideally it should be viewed first from the terrace of the main church, San Giorgio, from where you look down over a patchwork of tiled roofs and a warren of narrow stone and dirt streets and stairways which seem like an inspiration for an Escher drawing. To the south-west rises the sharp point of Dosso Alto; to the north-east that of Monte Carena. With an alpine feel about it, Bagolino in some ways resembles villages in the Valtellina and stacks of neatly-cut logs indicate the same concern for the onset of winter. Bagolino always seems busy. Somewhere there are the sounds of a hammer, a saw, or the mixing of plaster, and at lunchtime and in the early evening the local cafés are crowded with workers (frequently all men . . .) who have taken time off for a glass or two of local wine. San Giorgio itself is a seventeenth-century church with a painted interior which includes an optical illusion. Where the barrel vault of the roof begins to curve, a series of pillars has been painted. If you stand in the centre of the aisle, beneath the fresco of the patron saint, they all appear perpendicular and create the impression of a gallery. Viewed from either end their angles are very different, but the principal effect is worthy of comparison with the illusion created by Bramante in San Satiro in Milan.

From Bagolino, a minor road eventually linking with the S42 runs north and then west to skirt the southern edge of the highest and most inaccessible of Lombardy's mountain regions, stretching south from

Lavenone, dominated by its parish church, just to the south of Lake Idro.

the Stelvio park. Here there are a number of testing walks, especially around the *rifugio* Rosa on the shores of the tiny, attractive Lago di Vacca. For the less ambitious, the road through the small skiing area above Gaver and over the 1892-metre pass at Croce Domini is well worth taking for the increasingly superb views on both sides.

This road comes down through Bienno, into the Val

Camonica, the upper stretch of which is the best known and most beautiful of Lombardy's valleys. Except occasionally, when the weather is very bad, it is also possible to turn south from the Passo di Croce Domini and drive along the crest of the mountains to Dasdana – from where there is a 2-kilometre walk to the small, pretty lakes at Ravenole – and the pass at Maniva. Thereafter the road south is easier and follows the Mella river through Collio, Bovegno and Gardone in the Val Trompia.

As bases for holidays and excursions, Collio and Bovegno are growing quickly but, it is sad to say, characterlessly. And despite some attractive water-falls, its local reputation and much publicity, the lower part of the Val Trompia has little to recommend it. The ice-grey river rushes down between woods that have all too clearly suffered from excessive exposure to carbon-monoxide. Quarries – some now abandoned – scar the hillside. Leave the S345 after Gardone and follow signs for Polaveno and then Iseo over the Passo di Tre Termini. To the south is the northernmost edge of the industrial belt that creeps up from Brescia, marked by machine-making plants, wood yards and cement works. But there are some fine sweeps of grassland and the road wanders pleasantly between beeches, oaks and poplars before zigzagging down to the lake. (The road east from Brozzo through Lodrino and eventually to Nozza is very similar.)

This descent to Lake Iseo demonstrates the drama of its position. More than any of the other lakes, the water gives the impression of being cupped between mountains pushed up by some huge force, and there are clearly evident fault lines in the face of the rocky promontory of the Corno di Predore on the western shore. From this distance, too, swampy green patches at the southern end of the lake appear to be paddy-fields. They are in fact a mixture of peat-bogs and pools and in the late spring and summer the open water is carpeted with water-lilies. The pools are also a famous breeding-ground for tench, which is usually grilled and served with *polenta* as a local speciality. Other fish, too, are widely available, among them perch, sardines, herrings and small fresh-water salmon. The fish markets at Iseo and Pisogne are excellent, and you can often see a catch being dried in the sun spread out on large racks.

Like Idro, Lake Iseo has suffered from having to provide for the summer visitor. Extensive camp sites cover parts of the shore around Iseo and at Vesto a few kilometres further north, and just outside Pisogne a huge white concrete model of a horse ensures that you are aware of one of the village's chief activities. But tourism has not yet spoilt the Monte Isola, which rises enticingly from the lake.

To visit the island, leave the main coast road (S510) at Sulzano and park by the minute information kiosk and harbour. Like Varenna on Lake Como, Sulzano is very much a lakeside village, cut off from through traffic. Every 15 minutes or so (and for 2300 lire) a ferry plies between it and Peschiera Maraglio on Monte Isola. There are also other boats which make longer trips and dozens of privately-owned fishing boats with outboard motors which buzz back and forth. Monte Isola is reputed to be the biggest lake island in Europe. From the 'mainland', it looks like a great cone, its rich green slopes splashed with the near black of cypress trees and in autumn with the purple of wild heather. Once there you may find that it does not quite match the romantic picture given by some brochures, which suggest that it is car-free and inhabited solely by painters and fishermen. Cars there may not be, but there are island buses and dozens of scooters parked near the ferry in neat rows awaiting the return of their owners. Fishing is important, but the main activity is making rope and nets, for all sorts of other occupations as well as fishing.

It takes about two hours to walk round the island on the path accompanying the perimeter road. There are also a number of steeper tracks crossing from one side to another which enable you to explore the island quite thoroughly and appreciate the varied plant life, which is protected; if you are lucky you will discover wild orchids. With a local map it is easy to combine a long walk with the island bus and visit most of Monte Isola in a good half-day. Refreshments are available in each of the villages! Two echoes from the island's past

Left Monte Isola and Lake Iseo under the threatening skies of autumn, seen across the clustered roofs of Tavernola.

Above Peschiera Maraglio, the largest village on Monte Isola, the conical island which dominates Lake Iseo.

117

Patterns in knots and colours: net-making is the traditional industry of Peschiera on Monte Isola.

are also interesting. The composer Chopin is said to have spent time here with his mistress George Sand, and nearly a century earlier that independent and intrepid eighteenth-century traveller, Lady Mary Wortley Montagu, wrote enthusiastically about it and indeed about the beauty of the whole lake when she went to Lovere ('the Tunbridge of this part of the world') for a cure in 1747.

From Sulzano, the S510 continues to the northern end of the lake and then follows the Oglio river into the Val Camonica. This can be divided into three distinct sections. Until just before Breno the valley is almost flat, cultivated with orchards, some vines and grain; around Cedegolo it begins to climb through wooded hills; towards Edolo and beyond to Tonale it becomes dramatically mountainous. The name of the valley is derived from that of an ancient tribe – the Comuni – whose existence is testified by engravings which have

been dated to 3000 BC. The biggest collection of these is to be seen in the Parco Nazionale delle Incisione Rupestri at Capo di Ponte, where one sheet of rock, the Grande Roccia di Naquane, is covered with an estimated 876 carvings, including many of weapons, tools, geometric signs and religious symbols. One of them, a four-leafed rose, has been adopted as Lombardy's emblem.

South of Capo di Ponte is Breno, an ideal place to leave the main road and interesting in itself. The parish church has a fine fifteenth-century tableau of Christ in the tomb, with a dog, unusually, included among the wooden figures, and a huge, ornate high altar flanked by blue-grey marble columns and topped by a cupola rising almost to the roof. In a side chapel there is a black marble altar decorated with skulls and crossbones – a similarly macabre reminder of man's mortality is to be seen in Clusone nearby (see p.121). A stiff climb leads to the fourteenth-century castle perched above the town to the south-west; before setting off, call in at the town hall where you can borrow the keys if the castle is not open. Once inside, visit the dungeons and notice how several houses, still inhabited, are built into the lower sections of the external walls. Another building worthy of note is the Villa Ghezza on the main road just north of the town centre, a nineteenth-century folly on a grandiose scale, built in Muslim style by a local explorer.

From Breno, branch west up the valley of the Trobiolo to Borno and beyond along the attractive road following the River Dezzo to the village of the same name. Climbing still higher, the road turns south and then west over the Passo della Presolana at a height of nearly 1300 metres before running down into Clusone 700 metres below.

Clusone is a large, prosperous village relying for its wealth on the clothing industry (there are twenty-five workshops) and tourism, and is an ideal centre from which to explore the whole region extending west

This war memorial in Breno could be taken for a cattle shed.

Left **Piles of newly-cut hay near Breno in the lower Val Camonica.**

Right **Details from the walls of the Villa Ghezza in Breno, an extraordinarily ornate building designed and built by a local explorer in the nineteenth century.**

from Lake Iseo. A population of about 8000 swells to over 20,000 in the summer and not many fewer in the winter-sports season, when people come here from Milan and Brescia. Evidence of the presence of ancient tribal, Roman and Carolingian settlements has been uncovered in and around Clusone, and there are patches of frescoes dating from the early twelfth century on the walls of the town hall in Piazza Sant' Andrea and on the arcaded Piazza dell'Orologio. In the latter, as its name indicates, is the town clock, a 24-hour, astrological instrument of great intricacy. Designed and built in 1538 by Pietro Fanzago, it has hardly had to be repaired since, and only one wheel, the ropes and stone weights have ever had to be replaced. If you

ask at the tourist office at the foot of the tower, you will be taken to see the mechanism in a loft above the new council chambers, where you will also see a sixteenth-century painting of Clusone showing many more taller buildings than there are today and a fountain in Piazza dell'Orologio. At the highest point of the village is the church of San Bernardino, more commonly known as the Oratorio dei Disciplini, its front façade still displaying a fifteenth-century fresco depicting the triumph of death, with each citizen being led by a skeleton to meet a skeleton Christ. Inside there is a life-size tableau of Christ in the tomb comparable with the one at Breno, and some beautiful fifteenth-century frescoes depict episodes from Christ's life, including

121

Left Clusane at the southern end of Lake Iseo is an ideal base for exploring both sides of the lake.

Above Intimations of mortality. Part of the *danse macabre* fresco in Clusone.

the Stations of the Cross. Although mundane in comparison, do notice the worn pine floor of this delightful little church.

While in Clusone, it is worth taking the opportunity to explore the valley of the Serio immediately to the north. The road is kept open except in the severest winter conditions and the prosperous little spa of Boario Terme in particular should be visited; four renowned springs here – Antica Fonte, Fausta, Silia and Igea – provide water for the treatment of liver diseases. The road also gives access to splendid walking country. An organized, seven-day tour leaves from Valcanale, just 6 kilometres off the main road, and follows a path north and east through an area dotted with tiny, pretty lakes below some of the highest peaks of the Orobie Alps. The region is rich in minerals and local people will tell you that gold and silver have been discovered in the past. In spring it is beautiful with the blossoms of rhododendrons and a huge variety of wild flowers.

Bergamo can be reached directly and quickly from Clusone along the valley of the Serio, but two other, far more spectacular routes have much more to offer. One drops back to Lake Iseo and Lovere across a series of farmed plateaux, and then follows the road skirting the edge of the lake to Sarnico. About 12 kilometres after Lovere, a steep side road twists up the mountainside to Vigolo, from where there are superb views over Monte Isola. The second route, to the north-west of the Serio, follows a series of tiny roads through Gorno and Dossena and then San Pellegrino, where it joins the main S470 running through Zogno into Bergamo. To the north lies the Val Brembana, dotted with ski resorts in winter, and beyond are the peaks of the Orobie Alps marking the boundary with the province of Sondrio. Even though some of the more remote roads are unsurfaced, there is no difficulty in negotiating them outside the winter months, and the area again offers a

variety of walks through beautiful grassland and woods for which information is widely available locally. A network of radio-telephones is currently being introduced so help can be summoned speedily in the event of an accident or difficulty. Seen from a distance, the machines look like red-and-white robots.

Old prints of Bergamo show it sitting proudly on its rock surrounded by desolate expanses of flat and in parts marshy land. The original tribal settlement here was captured in AD 200 by the Romans, who named it Bergomum. The position was fortified and the extent of the Roman town was probably that of the old city today. Parts of the original walls can be seen. Sacked by Germanic tribes after the Romans left, Bergamo redeveloped in the Middle Ages, becoming an important centre for local government and for commercial activity. Approached from any direction, but especially from the south, the advantages of its position can still be sensed, though the plain has been taken over by industry, agriculture and an airport. The medieval town, Bergamo Alta, is 150 metres or so above the largely nineteenth-century Bergamo Bassa. The flank of the hill on which it sits sweeps round in a graceful curve, its south-facing slopes either intensively cultivated or smoothly green with the terraced lawns surrounding fashionable villas. Mrs Piozzi chose to compare it with the elegant sweep of 'Lansdown Road at Bath'.

So well publicized and known is the old town of Bergamo that there is a tendency to neglect Bergamo Bassa, though it too has its medieval parts, in particular to the south-west around the church of San Alessandro. There are also elegant boulevards, expensive apartments and villas, smart shops, terraced restaurants and the town's theatre, the Teatro Donizetti (named after the composer), in Piazza Giacomo Matteotti.

From this square, you can walk up Viale Vittorio Emanuele II to the foot of the escarpment and the funicular railway which will take you to the *città alta*. Immediately you step from the carriage you notice a change in atmosphere. The university, a large seminary and a school, together with Bergamo's college of

---

Giuseppe Garibaldi, the architect of Italy's unification, gazes steadfastly from his pedestal in Lovere.

Left The delicacy of the wood carving on these door panels in San Martino, Sarnico, is remarkable and among the best in the region.

Right The church of Santa Grata in the old quarter of Bergamo, the *città alta*, is tucked down a side street.

music (which also houses the Donizetti museum) provide a steady flow of young people. There are almost always tourists here and the main streets are full of tempting pastry and bread shops, restaurants, cafés and one particularly good wine bar. In the early evening, and especially when the weather is fine, local residents are much in evidence buying provisions for their evening meal and enjoying an aperitif before night closes in. In winter, however, when the wind can blow with some force from the north, the old town seems completely isolated, and, as in Mortara or Vigevano in western Lombardy, you are reminded just how isolated such communities once were, and how the inhabitants must have felt compelled to withdraw inside their city walls for safety.

The principal historic buildings of Bergamo Alta are conveniently clustered around Piazza Vecchia and Piazza Duomo. The fifteenth-century cathedral, considerably restored in the seventeenth century, is a very bright building with much white plaster, gilt ornamentation and pale marble. Immediately on the left inside the west door is the Eucharist chapel with a double cupola roof which appears (as indeed it should) to soar into the infinite; it was decorated by Giovanni Tiepolo in the eighteenth century in characteristically delicate pastel shades. Just across the corner of the square are the church of Santa Maria Maggiore, an outstanding example of twelfth-century craftsmanship, and the adjoining Cappella Colleoni, dating from 300 years later.

Santa Maria Maggiore's north door is flanked by slim, pink marble columns – rising from the backs of lions like those at the entrance to Lodi cathedral – which support an arch carved with hunting scenes. Statues of the Virgin and attendant saints stand in two open galleries above. If seen alone, this would rank as a fine entrance, but it is reduced to virtual insignificance by the adjoining façade of the chapel. Designed by the sculptor Giovanni Amadeo, it is largely constructed of delicately worked and decorated pink marble and justly ranks amongst the finest pieces of renaissance architecture anywhere in Italy. The whole building was commissioned by Bartolomeo Colleoni as his own funerary monument and as a tribute to the region where he lived and fought, and he had an existing building demolished in order to make way for it. Today Colleoni would probably be regarded as a high-class mercenary, but there seems to be no doubt about his military skills and ingenuity, which were rewarded by those in the highest positions, including Pope Paul II.

Begun in 1472, the sarcophagus was not completed until 1476, a year after Colleoni's death, and the intricacy of the work achieved in those four years almost defies belief. Colleoni's fame – and opinion of himself – are reflected in a series of allegorical allusions. Joshua is there, rubbing shoulders with Hercules – from whom Colleoni considered himself to be directly descended – Samson and Roman emperors. Colleoni seems to have considered his qualities as a leader to be divinely inspired, and probably without equal, his egocentricity and ostentation matching, if not surpassing, those of d'Annunzio (see p.110).

You can sometimes pass directly into Santa Maria Maggiore from this monument to self-aggrandizement, but the interconnecting door is usually locked and it is necessary to go outside again and enter the church by the north or south door (where lions again support the porch). The richness of the interior decoration is overwhelming. Overhead ornate plasterwork sets off paintings of angels interspersed with medallions depicting scenes from the Bible. Most of the walls are covered with tapestries from Tuscany and Holland, adding to a sumptuous heaviness which is in sharp contrast to the atmosphere in the cathedral. Remains of fourteenth-century frescoes still survive on the walls, a depiction of the Last Supper to the north and across the church a painting of the baby Jesus being circumcised.

For a complete change from such ecclesiastical intensity, leave Piazza Vecchia by Via Colleoni and turn into Vicolo Sant'Agata. This is a dead-end, but about half-way along is a kind of working-men's club

Outside one of the side chapels of Bergamo cathedral.

Left Animals, knights and peasants sculpted in Bergamo cathedral.

Above Light and shade between cathedral and Santa Maria Maggiore in Bergamo Alta.

131

with snooker tables, a garden cultivated with fruit and vegetables, and a pair of bowling alleys. The noisy and welcoming atmosphere here is quite different from that found anywhere else in Bergamo Alta, and it is a splendid place to go for hot wine on a cold winter's afternoon.

It is similarly refreshing to stroll through the botanical gardens or around the perimeter of the old town to enjoy the views, or in summer to sit in the shade of the chestnut trees or simply wander at random through the network of alleys, small squares and covered passages. The composer Gaetano Donizetti (1797–1848) was born in Bergamo and the museum named after him displays the wood and brass instruments used for the first performance of his first opera, *Enrico di Borgogna*, produced in Venice in 1818. Also to be noted are the house where Stendhal once stayed, the former public washing-place just nearby in Via Mario Lupo and the tomb of the Agosti family, benefactors of Bergamo in the seventeenth century. Now incongruously placed in the town library in Piazza Vecchia, the tomb is fronted by two marble lions gazing heavenwards.

The octagonal baptistery opposite the cathedral in Bergamo. The white lines in the foreground are part of an intriguing calendar.

The funicular awaits those who prefer not to walk (cars not belonging to residents are unceremoniously towed away), but the south-east side of the hill is gentle enough. Walking in this direction also has the advantage of taking you to the art gallery, the Accademia Carraro, a severe, early nineteenth-century neo-classical *palazzo* where the much vaunted collection is particularly rich in work by Lombard and Venetian artists. My two favourite pictures here hang side by side, one by Giovanni Bellini, the other by Mantegna. They are both of the Madonna and Child, but whereas Mantegna's Jesus is still very much an infant – shown looking heavenwards in some distress – Bellini has painted a sturdy little boy who gives the impression of struggling to free himself from his mother's arms. The contrast is simple but effective.

Finally, Bergamo excels in a feature of domestic Lombard architecture which I have not seen so elegantly exploited anywhere else, even in Milan. Typically, the houses have massive doors on to the street. Inside, there is a second, usually of wrought iron, leading to one or more *cortili*, with a light hanging above. This design applies to large and small residences alike, giving a particularly acute sense of going *into* the building. To see how this can be used to considerable effect in a commercial area, visit nos. 19 and 23 in Via Pignolo near the church of San Satiro in Bergamo Bassa. And sample the cakes in no. 23.

4
Lake Como and the Valtellina

Monza – the Brianza – Bellagio – Como – Lecco –
Menaggio – Lake Lugano – Gravedona – Chiavenna –
Madesimo – Spluga pass – Sondrio – Tirano – Bormio –
Ponte di Legno – Edolo

The northern part of Lombardy, which pushes up into Switzerland, is dominated by lakes Como and Lecco, and by the mountainous Valtellina. The latter, which derives its name from Val Teglio, a village just west of Tirano that was important in the Middle Ages, is crossed by two major valleys, both natural communication routes now followed by road and rail. The first, the Valchiavenna, runs north from Lake Como along the rivers Mera and Liro and through the Spluga pass to Switzerland. The second follows the valley of the Adda east for 60 kilometres to Tirano, after which it curves northwards to the river's source in the lake of San Giacomo di Fraele in the Stelvio national park. This is the northernmost point of the province, overlooked by the massive peaks of the Cima Paradiso and the Cassa del Ferro. Well over 80 per cent of the region is above 1000 metres and away from the two main valleys exploration becomes as challenging as it is rewarding.

No one visiting this part of Lombardy, however, can fail to notice the effects of the disastrous landslide of 28 July 1987 at San Antonio Morignone, a village 10 kilometres east of Sondalo in the upper Adda valley. Excessive rain in the previous weeks had caused the Adda and its tributaries to swell to unprecedented levels, undermine the steep valley sides and create a natural dam of debris. A new lake formed which, after more rain, threatened to burst its banks and pour down towards Sondalo and Tirano. Fortunately this never happened, but as a precaution over 25,000 people were evacuated to higher, safer villages for several weeks. Eventually the waters subsided, but the damage to property had been very considerable. For crude economic reasons, it was essential that access to the skiing area to the north-east around Bormio should be possible by the beginning of the winter season. Such was the determination and skill of the civil engineers that by early December millions of tonnes of earth and rock had been moved and kilometres of piping and concrete reinforcement laid. The result is literally a new mountainside – grey, stony and inhospitable – crossed by a road which winds through more than twenty hairpin bends. On a fine summer's day it demands caution; when there is wind, rain or snow, it is positively frightening. Yet no matter what care is taken to ensure, as far as this is possible, that such a catastrophe will not occur again, the raw, new mountain will remain as a monument to one of the worst natural disasters in Europe for a long time. The full ecological consequences will not be apparent for years, even decades, but the social ones have been immediate. Fortunately relatively few people were killed, but about 500 have lost either home or land (and therefore livelihood), or both, as a result of the disaster. A local committee has been set up in an attempt to stimulate government action; tourists are asked to sign petitions and photographs of the disaster are sold to raise both money and the level of public awareness. Graffiti accusing the authorities of cynicism and inaction have already appeared on rock faces and concrete slabs. And just by the side of the road to the north of the new pass is a powerful and macabre reminder of what happened. On an outcrop of rock above the valley stands the church of San Bartolomeo, miraculously saved from destruction by its position. Just inside the main porch is an ossuary containing the bones recovered from local cemeteries. A notice reminds you that there are others now buried deep beneath the surface of the new mountain which are lost forever.

This northern section of Lombardy is easily reached from Milan by both road and rail, north-west to Como or north-east to Lecco. The road joining these towns runs attractively between a series of much smaller lakes and the first foothills of the mountains separating the lower reaches of Como and Lecco just to the north.

To the south is the Brianza, a wedge of land like an inverted triangle with its apex towards Milan. For the most part – especially immediately north of Milan – it is uninteresting, with much light industry (in particular furniture making), gravel-workings and pockets of low-budget housing. But there are places to note. From Montevecchia about 20 kilometres south of Lecco, just to the west of the original S36, there are splendid panoramic views over much of the region; 5 kilometres to the south-east are Cernusco, with a magnificent sixteenth-century house, and Merate, with the classically proportioned Villa Belgioioso and an observatory which is open to the public once a month. And there is Monza, internationally known for its motor-racing circuit in the 800-hectare Parco on the north side of the city. Here too are a polo pitch and golf courses, additional facilities for rich *milanesi*. The park was originally laid out in 1806 around the classical Villa Reale, built in the late eighteenth century for Archduke Ferdinand of Austria and set off by magnificent gardens with clumps of mature trees and wandering paths. Because of its present-day attractions, the park is frequently busy, but it is glorious in the spring and offers many quiet spots for picnics. One wing of the villa is now an art gallery housing a fine collection of eighteenth- and nineteenth-century work by local artists, especially Mose Bianchi (1840–1904).

The old, self-contained part of the town, which dates from the fifth century, is centred on the cathedral of San Giovanni Battista and the thirteenth-century Palazzo Arengario. The former, also dating from the thirteenth century but not finished until the nineteenth, has a striking west front in green and white marble. Six pinnacled turrets rising from the façade accentuate the outlines of the building. Inside, the chapels flanking the aisles are mostly interconnected, making the building seem much bigger than it actually is. Visitors can also see the cathedral treasure, including the *corona del ferro*, or iron crown, so called on account of the thin strip of iron which runs round the much broader band of gold and which is said to have been made from a nail from Christ's cross.

The lakes are reached most quickly from Milan by the main roads to Como and Lecco. Between them is a triangular wedge of attractive mountainous country which pushes up north between the lakes. To the south, this area is again almost cut off by water, bordered by a chain of small, shallow lakes – Montorfano, Alserio, Pusiano, Segrino and Annone – running between Como and Lecco. Two in particular have interesting stories connected with them. Montorfano is said to have once contained a species of carp which grew to an abnormally large size and was regarded as a local delicacy, while in 1820 Pusiano was the first lake in Italy to be navigated by a steam ship.

At the northern tip of the wedge is the resort of Bellagio, reached by lakeside roads tucked in under steep, tree-covered slopes where a number of elegant

Absent friends in Urio, Lake Como.

residences enjoy views across the water. To the west, the peaks of Monte Bisbino and Sasso Gordona mark the boundary with Switzerland and attractive villages dot the far shore of the lake. To the east, the view is more dramatic, with mountains several hundred metres higher. In summer the lakes are busy with boats of all shapes and sizes and there are a number of camp sites and attractive lakeside areas popular with tourists and locals alike. Less frequented but more interesting is the inland route to Bellagio, along the valley of the River Lambro, the Vallassina. Less than a century ago this area could only be explored on foot or horseback.

From a cluster of roads just to the west of Pusiano the route to Bellagio cuts up by way of Canzo (a centre of knife manufacturing) to Asso. To the west, the flanks of Monte Palanzone, attractively wooded with clumps of oaks, chestnuts and birches, rise to nearly 1500 metres. Just over the ridge is a *rifugio* and various paths run down to Lake Como at Pognana and Torno. Similarly, a number of *rifugi* and tracks across wooded slopes to the east make this an area easily explored on foot. It is also possible to take a narrow road from Asso to Maisano, or west through Zelbio. This tiny village sheltering under the southern face of Monte San Primo is noted in spring for its dazzling displays of wild narcissi. Thereafter the road winds steeply down to Nesso where a stream (known here, as in other similar places, as the *orrido*) rushes through a narrow, sinister gorge into the lake.

Six kilometres beyond the Zelbio turn-off, a small road on the left cuts up to Cernobbio and the magnificent sixteenth-century Villa d'Este (transformed into a hotel in 1873 to cater for an increasing tourist trade). Superb gardens are noted especially for an avenue of cypress trees leading up to high ground behind the house and to a series of artificial waterways. Bellagio on its wooded, rocky promontory is reached within minutes from here. Undeniably beautiful and magnificently set — its name derives from *bi-lacus*, between the lakes — it attracts tourists in their thousands. A number of elegant and expensive hotels and the ferry port to the west are backed by narrow

stepped streets leading to Via Garibaldi and the restored twelfth-century church of San Giacomo at its northern end, with fine fifteenth-century altars. The municipal park and gardens just below are bright with flowering shrubs and trees in spring but do not match the grandeur of the parkland of the medieval Villa Serbelloni (completely restored in the eighteenth century and now a conference and study centre), which falls away steeply to the east. Paths and granite stairways lead down to the tiny port known as the Punta Spartievento at the northern end of the peninsula and to Castello Sfondrata on the east. The views are perhaps at their best in winter, when the mountains just to the south are often dusted with snow and the light is especially bright.

By comparison with Bellagio, both Como and Lecco are large and anonymous. Como, at the foot of the 900-metre Monte Brunate (which can be reached by funicular railway), has sprawled inland and has understandably taken advantage of its superb natural position. Today it is a busy cultural, commercial and tourist centre, much in demand for conferences; many of these are held in the Villa Olmo just to the west of the town, a superb late eighteenth-century classical house set in fine parkland running down to the lake.

For all its modernity, Como has long historic associations. Iron Age remains have been discovered here and it was the site of a series of Gallic tribal settlements until the Romans occupied it and gave it the name from which its present one is derived, Novum Comun. Much later, in the eighteenth century, Como became popular as a summer resort with the Milanese aristocracy. Many legacies of this historic past can be seen in the small, central section of the town, laid out on an original Roman grid plan, only five minutes' walk across Piazza Cavour from the harbour. Here the cathedral and *broletto* give on to the well-proportioned market square with a large selection of cafés to choose from. The *broletto*, decorated in grey,

A strained Pliny the Younger robed and seated in splendour outside Como cathedral.

white and red marble and with an open arcade on the ground floor, was begun in the thirteenth century, though the balcony from which proclamations would be read was not added until the fifteenth. A number of amusing, tiny faces are carved on the frieze of small arches half-way up the front of the building.

Santa Maria Maggiore, which resembles the cathedral at Monza, was begun at the very end of the fourteenth century and completed – with the addition of the dome at the east end – nearly 200 years later. A rose window punctuating the soaring, pinnacled west façade, tapestries, and an octagonal font all date from the sixteenth century. Other features include a seventeenth-century pulpit and organ front, superb baroque chapels celebrating the Virgin (south transept) and the Adoration of Christ (north), and a modern (1940) episcopal throne. And try, too, to be in the cathedral when the light is from the east. A small window high in the apse offers a lens-like image of the very top of Monte Brunate. At the west end on the south side is a dwarf effigy of Mary Magdalene in a glass case, while the eleventh-century tomb of Bishop Julius across the church is primitively carved with Christian symbols – fishes and a slaughtered lamb.

Of the other half-dozen churches in this central area, the twelfth-century San Fedele, in Via Vittorio Emanuele, is on the site of the original fifth-century cathedral. This intimate, ornate, galleried building with some fine thirteenth-century frescoes is rather like a small Orthodox church. About a kilometre to the south, and also on the site of a fifth-century church, is the eleventh-century Sant'Abbondio, where the crypt contains the tombs of some of the former bishops of Como.

Somehow, however, the modern world seems particularly intrusive in this ancient part of Como, even if it does have its own attractions. In the public gardens overlooking the lake there is a striking modern

The grandiose temple to Alessandro Volta, inventor of the electric battery and Como's most celebrated citizen of the last two centuries.

monument to peace, a war memorial – the Monumento in Caduti by the futurist architect Antonio Sant'Elia – and the neo-classical Tempio Voltiano, built in 1927 and dedicated to Alessandro Volta (1745–1827), the inventor of the modern electric battery. Here, too, the local people come to fish, play cards or simply wander, especially in the spring and summer, when there are fresh breezes off the lake. The two prevailing winds, the *tivano* from the north and the *breva* from the south, have encouraged the development of sailing and wind-surfing, but at times they blow strongly enough to be quite unpleasant. The lake is also the source of a variety of fish, including eels, trout and perch. But despite this and the abundance of mushrooms, there are no really typical local dishes. As though conscious of their town's international appeal, the people of Como seem to have opted for a satisfying but unremarkable common denominator acceptable to Milanese businessmen and American and Japanese tourists alike. And that is a pity.

Lecco, 25 kilometres to the east at the base of its own lake, is also an important tourist and commercial centre with some industry. It does not, however, have Como's national and international dimensions and exists rather in the shadow of its more illustrious neighbour, which is about twice as large. Nor is Lecco so rich in historic buildings. But the narrow, vaulted streets immediately off the main lakeside road have retained their charm and to the east of the centre is the Villa Manzoni, now part of the town's museum, where the novelist lived for some time as a boy. The rooms on the ground floor contain some interesting records of his later activities – manuscripts, private papers and first editions; a collection of Italian paintings from the seventeenth century to the present day is hung on the floor above.

From Como, Lecco or Bellagio you can make a complete circuit of the lakes by road, or, more interestingly, work out a route which incorporates some of the ferry crossings. By comparison with the usual costs of Italian transport these are not particularly cheap, but they are better value than the boat trips for tourists. They also have the attraction of a

Left Lierna, Lake Lecco.

Above In many lakeside communities, white-washed houses rise directly from the water. This is Brienno on Lake Como.

143

genuine Italian atmosphere as people go about their everyday lives commuting to work or visiting relatives. And they provide some of the best views of the lakeside villas and gardens, which are often hidden from the roads above them.

Just west of Como a fast new road cut into the side of the hill takes you quickly north to Menaggio. But it is better to leave this main route at Cernobbio and pick your way along the original road linking a string of tiny, delightful, self-contained villages as far as Torriggia. Here, despite the undoubted wealth brought by tourism, you will find local people still pursuing their living in traditional ways. They may be somewhat surprised that you have not chosen to bypass them on the upper road! Cernobbio itself has a number of imposing villas, Carate is overlooked by the remains of a medieval castle and there is a most impressive monumental cemetery at Laglio. Twenty kilometres further north at Tremezzo is the eighteenth-century Villa Carlotta, now a botanical museum. It was originally called the Villa Clerici, but was renamed in the mid nineteenth century when it was bought by Princess Carlotta of Prussia. It was she who planted the romantic garden on the lake shore, while near the house a formal eighteenth-century garden descends in steep terraces to the lake. The gardens are full of exotic trees and shrubs from all over the world, including tree ferns and giant redwoods, and are at their best in April and May when the azaleas are in full flower. From the lake they look magnificent.

At Argegno, almost exactly half-way between Cernobbio and Menaggio, a minor road cuts up over the mountains and down to Lake Lugano. As the road climbs, the vegetation changes. The exotic Mediterranean bushes and trees of the lakeside give way to northern European species, such as beech. Valleys are thickly wooded, but there is also some grassland and the whole area is good walking country. From San

Tremezzo on the western shore of Lake Como, an ideal point from which to explore the hinterland or to begin an excursion by ferry.

The gardens of the Villa Carlotta on Lake Como are famous for displays of spring flowers.

Fedele d'Intelvi marked paths lead north through Laino and Ponna down to Claino overlooking Lake Lugano. These attractive villages with narrow streets and diminutive squares are a little off the main tourist routes. But they have their problems. In Claino, for example, such is the danger from vandalism that the two village churches have had to be closed and their monuments removed to Milan for safe-keeping.

The road from Claino reaches the lake at Osteno, a pretty fishing village popular with *milanesi*, who have invested in holiday homes, and with campers. The village has a pleasant atmosphere and the view northwest across the lake from the tiny harbour is especially fine. The hills fringing the water rise steeply to over 1000 metres and are covered with large patches of chestnut and oak woods. In autumn, when the leaves turn red and gold, the slopes become a blaze of colour and are all the more attractive when there is an early

Above The Villa Carlotta, Lake Como, is set off by a formal garden descending in steep terraces to the lake.

Right Symmetry and eroticism combined at the Villa Carlotta.

A peaceful, classical welcome to one of the water gardens at the Villa Carlotta.

fall of snow. Nearer the lakeside are vines and clumps of hellebore, whose white blossoms contrast sharply in winter with the dark branches and piles of dead leaves. From Osteno, a ferry crosses the water to San Mamete on the north side, from where it is less than 4 kilometres to Oria, the last village before the border with Switzerland and no more than a few houses clustered around a church and some cypress trees. On the southern edge of the lake the road back east from Osteno passes an unremarkable grotto and waterfall at Rescia.

At the eastern end of the lake there are some sandy beaches, but access is reserved for those using the camp sites here. Further round, in the village of Porlezza, there are stony beaches leading to deeper water that is more suitable for sailing. Porlezza itself is an ideal point to break a journey into Switzerland, or to use as a base for some demanding walks into the steep mountains immediately to the north. A map posted in the village indicates the *sentiero delle quattro valli* (way of the four valleys), reached by driving directly north to Cavargna, a remote village perched over 1000 metres up on the south-west slopes of Monte Tabor. From here the path south to Dasio is reasonably well marked, and a more interesting route runs south-east by way of the Val Cavargna and the Alpe Erba, winding steeply across the face of Monte Grona before dropping down into Breglia. Just west of the village, at a height of about 1400 metres, is a *rifugio* for those in need of a break!

The road from Porlezza completing the loop back to Lake Como runs past the small and attractive Lago di Piano and across a swampy and partly cultivated plateau with mountains on either side. Two kilometres or so before Menaggio it drops abruptly through several hairpin bends, with a series of splendid views of the tightly-packed roofs of the old town.

Backed by a great sweep of mountains, Menaggio is superbly situated. The village, much of which is on a promontory, looks south to Bellagio and east to Varenna, both of which can be reached by regular ferries. The atmosphere is almost always fresher than in Como and the community is lively and bustling, benefiting from the constant flow of traffic along the lakeside and through to Lugano and Switzerland. It is an ideal base for exploring the lake area.

The road from here 25 kilometres north to Gravedona passes through a series of villages, pretty in themselves but too often scarred by sprawling camp sites. Unquestionably the best way to appreciate this part of the lake, if you have the patience and time, is to take a series of boat trips zigzagging across the water as far as Calozzo and thereafter looping along the western shore to the most northerly harbour at Gera Lario. Whatever mode of transport you use, do not fail to see the medieval castle dominating the lake at

Looking north-east towards the promontory of Rezzonico on the west shore of Lake Como and beyond to Dervio and Monte Legnoncino.

Rezzonico – a village which takes its name from the family who built one of the most sumptuous palaces on the Grand Canal in Venice – and the stately *palazzo* at Dongo before stopping at Gravedona.

This is the largest of the villages in this area and, despite some light industry (paper and tiles), arguably the most attractive, with a well-restored centre. Steep medieval streets open on to a pleasant lakeside area where people fish and in the early morning queue for the daily papers. A red water-mill with its wheel still in place stands in Via Sugnappa and a handsome eighteenth-century house is at the lake end of the same street. Just to the north is an alley with a tiny chapel tucked away intimately at the far end; double doors and a grille in another opposite the landing-stage are a reminder that it was, and still is, possible to seal off whole sections of the village. These hidden back streets are worth exploring. One, just off the main square, leads to a tiny inner courtyard decorated with a fresco of the martyrdom of St Sebastian. In another, on a day in mid August, I once discovered a house with its lights on and an open fire burning strongly.

From Gravedona, Como can easily be reached in under an hour by doubling back along the west side of the lake. Continuing north takes you across the marshy Piano di Spagna – justly renowned for its birdlife, in particular different kinds of waders and ducks and the swans which are bred here – and along the S36 towards Colico from the confusing junction at Sant'Agata. This is popular tourist country with numerous, fully-equipped camp sites. But there are also some substantial private houses whose gardens are landscaped to the water's edge and whose owners can fish in privacy from their own verandas, a pastime which, according to his letters, Pliny the Younger also enjoyed. Once past Laghetto just a couple of kilometres south of Colico, however, camp sites fade away. Beaches are small and quiet even at the height of summer, several

Dongo, on the western shore of Lake Como. Early morning is the best time to experience these tiny villages.

Delicate plasterwork setting off a potted plant is typical of the kind of architectural detail found in Lombardy. This scene is in Gravedona.

of them reachable only by paths. The hills drop steeply into the water, with a series of tunnels carrying the railway which runs parallel to the road for the full length of the lake. To the east is the rugged area of the Valsassina reached by roads following the valleys of the Varrone, Pioverna and Esino. This is a popular region with walkers, offering a series of interlinking paths and well-equipped *rifugi*, some at nearly 2000 metres. Seven-day tours involving walks of five hours per day are organized by the official guides in Lecco; one of these, the principal route, goes as far as the 2554-metre Pizzo dei Tre Signori, from which views in all directions are quite magnificent.

The more sedentary can admire the mountains from afar and continue down the coast; only those in a hurry should use the expressway, nearly all tunnelled through the rock, which runs the full length of the east side of the lake. No one should miss Varenna. Park at the northern end of the village by the ferry stage and the seedy-looking but good Albergo Olivedo and walk back to the tiny harbour. You will pass a magnificent house with a Palladian façade high on your left, with gardens, including a grotto, tumbling down to the lake. (When I was there it was being guarded by a huge Dobermann. . . .) The main part of the village clings to the hillside above the water, cut by narrow alleys shaded by overhanging roofs and balconies, some of which join to bridge the street. In the very corner of the harbour, at the junction of Riva Garibaldi and Riva dei Marmisti, I watched a cooper and pail-maker demonstrate his skills. After the harbour – and maybe a drink – you can follow the path up to the village centre and the church of San Giorgio with its fourteenth-century frescoes. To the right as you climb is the Villa Monastero, built on the site of a thirteenth-century monastery and set off by beautiful lawns and rock gardens.

Because cars are kept out of the lakeside area, Varenna gives the impression of being a boating community. Its small bay is sheltered from most winds and at night the harbour is pleasantly illuminated, but the best time to be there is at dusk, with the sun setting to the west across the lake and the lights of Bellagio and Menaggio appearing one by one. No other village on this stretch of coast has quite the same charm. It is also worth driving up to the ruins of Castello Vezio high above the village, from where the views are extremely fine. The castle itself was said to have been founded by a Lombard queen, Theodolinda, who is supposed to have donated the iron crown to the cathedral at Monza.

As well as this complete circuit of the lakes, there are two rewarding excursions into the mountains from the northern tip of Como. One follows the Chiavenna towards the Spluga pass; the other runs east along the valley of the Adda to the Stelvio national park.

From the junction at Sant'Agata, the S36 to the north skirts the eastern edge of Lake Mezzola through Verceia and Novate Mezzola, a resort packed with tourists and campers in the summer months and best avoided. Cross the river just before Somaggia and follow the minor road linking a series of villages tucked in between the foot of the tree-covered mountains forming the border with Switzerland and a fertile plain given over primarily to the cultivation of maize and tobacco. Era, San Andrea, Samolaco and San Pietro are all worth visiting, tiny, compact communities huddled around their churches and the remains of former castles. Gordona, slightly bigger than the others, is being vigorously restored and is clearly a place for second homes. It marks the beginning of the exquisitely beautiful Bodengo valley which can be reached only along forest tracks, the details of which are shown on a map posted in the main square behind the church. Gordona is also said to be famed for its bread, but I failed to find a single bakery. From here north to Chiavenna, steel hoops preventing parking on the left-hand side of the road are a reminder of how busy this area is in the skiing season.

Chiavenna has benefited considerably from its location on the road to St Moritz. It is a friendly town, which has preserved many of its historic streets, tiny squares and seventeenth-century town houses. A beautifully plain twelfth-century font stands in the church of San Lorenzo. But commercialism has also made its mark here. The land on which Chiavenna is built is full of caves and pot-holes, known locally as *crotti* and for long used as cellars for storing local wines, cheeses and hams. Many of them have been transformed into wine bars and restaurants, and the boisterous holiday known as the Sagra dei Crotti in mid September is now a tourist attraction.

The bleak, inhospitable Spluga road, built by the Austrians between 1819–21 as a commercial route, opening up central Europe, winds north out of the town along the glacial valley of San Giacomo and rises to over 2100 metres at the border with Switzerland. It is frequently closed during severe weather in the

The ferry from Bellano, Lake Como. The houses set on the slopes high above can be reached only by a mule track.

Above **Varenna,** *village lacustre* **and perhaps the most attractive place on the eastern shore of Lake Como.**

Right **Autumn sun in a corner of the delightful gardens of the Villa Monastero, Varenna.**

Above **Patterns in wood and stone in the Val Chiavenna.**

Right **The houses of Chiavenna rise steeply on the slopes overlooking the River Mera. Swollen by melting snow in spring, the river turns into a torrent.**

winter months. To west and east the mountainsides are thickly wooded and you have to take the chair-lifts to reach the open spaces beyond the tree-line above Madesimo. From December to March the slopes are dotted with thousands of brightly-clothed skiers, who find it marginally cheaper to ski here than in Bormio or in Switzerland. Just north of Chiavenna, at San Giacomo Filippo, is an austere twelfth-century church, while a seventeenth-century sanctuary at Gallivaggio is said to commemorate the appearance of the Virgin Mary on 10 October 1492 to two children who were collecting chestnuts here. Fifteen kilometres further on, the wooden houses in the village of Isola, just off the main road, are worth a detour. There are opportunities for walks on both sides of the valley – through Olmo to Lago di Truzzo to the west, for example, or from Campodolcino through Fraciscio to the Angeloga pass at the southern end of the Valle di Lei to the east. None of these routes is long, but they are all dramatic, and the *rifugio* at the end can be a welcome sight. The paths are normally open all year, but June and September are the best months for exploring this area.

Along the Bregaglia valley in the direction of St Moritz, two stops are imperative: the first to visit the sixteenth-century Palazzo Vertemate-Franchi, just 3 kilometres from Chiavenna, with its beautiful frescoes by the Campi brothers from Cremona, ornate, inlaid ceilings and Italianate gardens planted with vines and chestnut trees; the second to walk up the steep steps which lead nearly 1000 metres from the waterfall (Acqua Fraggia) in Borgonuovo to the ancient but well-preserved village of Savogno, with its wooden houses and uneven stone alleyways.

Only at Sondrio, the provincial capital of the Valtellina some 40 kilometres from the northern end of Como, and at Ardenno, half-way between the two, is there any real access to the mountains between the Val

Bregaglia, followed by the S37, and the valley of the Adda followed by the S38. Less than 20 kilometres east of Sondrio is Tirano, an ideal base and only minutes from the Swiss border. Beyond here the S38 bisects the north-eastern corner of Lombardy, running along the western border of the Stelvio national park. All this area can be covered quite easily within a few hours and even from the main road there is a good impression of the variety of the terrain, with views to villages dominated by disproportionately large churches. Most of the cultivable land on the lower slopes – up to 800 metres or so – is covered by a patchwork of vineyards, often reached only by mule-tracks. Above, the hillsides are thickly wooded. A year after the disaster, the alluvial bed of the Adda valley was being recultivated and houses damaged by the flood restored.

Although some maize is grown, apples and the vine dominate this part of the valley. After the floods, conditions for rice were ideal, but it was rejected after a brief experiment. Many of the orchards are owned by Swiss concerns and in October huge quantities of perfect apples, each one apparently individually polished, begin their journey to enormous fruit co-operatives and then across the world. The vineyards have often belonged to the same family for generations. The slopes on which the vines are grown can be unbelievably steep and those who tend them or pick the grapes are often attached by rope to a fence or roadside barricade for safety. Machinery is moved and baskets of grapes are pulled up with the aid of a series of pulleys. To me it seems odd that the vines are planted in lines running *with* and not *across* the slope, an arrangement which aids drainage but, more significantly, would seem to encourage erosion of the soil. The kiwi fruit was also introduced here in the early 1980s, though it is yet to be extensively grown. The fact that the plant takes about five years to mature coupled with the high risk of theft once the fruit is ready have so far discouraged potential growers.

Above the vines, oaks and chestnuts gradually give way to pines and larches with a tangled undergrowth of brambles, rhododendrons and ferns. Amongst them you find hidden valleys and plateaux, in spring rich

Rocks shattered and eroded by the harsh climate border the Spluga pass leading north from Lombardy into Switzerland.

with wild flowers and in summer at haymaking heavy with the scent of camomile. *Baíte* are scattered across the hillsides, some neat, others almost in ruins. Some have been maintained as country retreats, but many still function as farmsteads. Chickens run wild, hay is stored in the loft and logs are neatly stacked ready for the winter.

To have access to this world, you have either to hunt out the dirt roads or to walk. Unless you are in a hurry to reach the Stelvio park, leave the S38 where it crosses the Piano di Spagna and join the S402 at Dubino; thereafter, follow the minor road which climbs up through a series of exceedingly tight hairpin bends and links the villages of Cino, Mello and Dazio, where it comes to an end overlooking a cemetery. From here it is necessary to go back to the Adda to reach Ardenno and the Masino valley running up to Bagni which, as the name implies, is known for its thermal baths. This beautifully situated village at a height of just over 1100 metres is surrounded by a great amphitheatre of mountains. To the west is the *rifugio* Omio, reached by a path known as the Roma which sweeps round north of Bagni before rejoining the road at Filorera. The route takes six days and involves climbing to over 2700 metres across the lower slopes of Monte Disgrazia. For experienced mountaineers equipped to undertake more hazardous climbs, it is possible to continue north-east and eventually join the Val Malenco at Chiareggio, 16 kilometres away.

To the east of Ardenno, the minor road running parallel to the S38 once more threads its way through a series of tiny, attractive villages, several of which, such as Berbenno and Sassella, are the homes of some of the better Valtellina wines. Just over half-way to Sondrio, it is worth making a deviation to Postalesio to see some curious rock formations like giant, elongated mushrooms. These are simply the result of wind erosion, but seem as if they might be remnants of a mysterious past or to have arrived from another planet.

The threatening waters of the Adda at Boffetto.

At Sondrio a few kilometres further east follow the road which parallels the Mallero river north to Chiesa and Caspoggio. This region is a skiing area and one of the richest sources of mineral wealth in Europe, with some magnificent deposits of quartz and serpentine, much used in semi-precious jewellery, as well as the more mundane slate. Consequently access is easy. As you climb towards the mountains, the village of Spriana with its stone houses perched at the foot of the forest on the east side of the valley comes into view. Within five kilometres you reach Chiesa, a busy village all the year round, and beyond it Primolo. Set on a terraced hillock against the backdrop of the Pizzo di Tre Mogge, this much smaller community enjoys one of the best positions in the whole region. Like the Val Masino, this area is popular with walkers in summer. You can join organized tours lasting up to a week which involve staying at some of the best equipped, oldest and most prestigious *rifugi* in Lombardy, such as those at Marinelli and Capanna Desio. After five or six hours' solid walking, a meal of local *bresaola*, salami and cheeses washed down by a fresh young wine from Sassella at one of these places is an experience that is not readily forgotten.

Caspoggio compares well with either Madesimo or Bormio. Like them, the village has developed as the result of winter sports, but it has done so in a different way. Madesimo, especially out of season, is a bland, plain place with no real atmosphere; Bormio is an all-year resort vying with the best in Switzerland and genuinely international. Caspoggio has retained its charm. Its old houses are being tastefully restored and new building has to date remained largely in character. As is the case with most ski resorts, it is interesting to be there in summer when the terrain is revealed and rocks and fences break up what in winter are vast areas of snow. And at this time of the year, too, those who become dashing, colourful ski instructors for three months or so are less romantically occupied in building, farming or shoe-making.

Sondrio itself, the focal point and capital of the Valtellina, is a bustling, rather large town by comparison with its immediate surroundings, but the old

Left Evening sunlight on Monte Legnone and the River Adda, here giving no hint of the raging torrent it can become.

Above The remote church of Ponte, buried deep in the wooded slopes of the Valtellina.

163

medieval quarter on the north side, trapped between the river and the hills, is quiet; here you can sit in Piazza Garibaldi and imagine the merchants, soldiers and pilgrims who have passed through for centuries. If you can, find an excuse to visit the municipal offices in the original sixteenth-century Palazzo Pretorio with its austere gateway and elegant courtyard, as well as the eighteenth-century church dedicated to saints Gervase and Prostase with two large paintings by Giacomo Parravicini (c.1660–1729) of their imagined martyrdom. The local museum in the early twentieth-century Palazzo Quadrio has an especially good collection of local arts and crafts.

Sondrio undoubtedly has its attractions and it is especially lively on a Saturday, when the large, weekly market is held. But, in my view, those looking for a base from which to explore the Valtellina would do better to continue along the valley to Tirano. Again, do not follow the S38 but keep to the smaller road to the north about 500 metres above the valley. As you approach Tirano, you will arrive at the major junction from which the S29 leads to Switzerland, always busy in the early morning with migrant workers or with people simply going to fill their petrol tanks with fuel that is two-thirds the price of what it costs in Italy! (The petrol station just 50 metres across the border never seems to be without customers.)

Modern-day Tirano is a thriving prosperous place. Ancient inscriptions carved in rocks indicate that man has lived here for thousands of years and, like Sondrio, Tirano has for centuries been an important 'frontier' town. There are a number of handsome *palazzi*, but by far the most significant building is the Santuario della Madonna, an imposing renaissance church at the west end of the main thoroughfare, the building of which was begun in 1505 to commemorate the appearance of the Virgin the year before. It is a place of pilgrimage still, and the small shrine behind the altar at the east end of the church is full of *ex-votos*, many of them modest family photographs put here in gratitude for

recovery from skiing accidents. The entire church is richly decorated, with much plasterwork and carved wood, and the upper walls and roof are painted with a mixture of religious scenes and non-figurative designs. The ornate seventeenth-century organ loft is held by many to be the finest in Lombardy and the church is regularly used for important recitals and concerts. The centre of the town is dominated by a 1980s shopping mall. Everywhere there is a sense of liveliness, and lying at an altitude of nearly 500 metres Tirano's climate is particularly agreeable.

From Tirano you can not only reach Switzerland by road or rail in a matter of minutes, but are also well placed for the Stelvio park, or for the S39 and S42 through Aprica and Edolo over the Tonale pass into Trentino. There are also paths into Switzerland, but these are now mostly overgrown. Even into the 1960s, however, they were used by smugglers who traded particularly in salt, coffee and matches. They worked in teams, with the leader (*caporello*) usually remaining safely behind and collecting the profits. This kind of self-help enterprise can be seen as a microcosm of the way local society as a whole works. The *valtellini* around Tirano have a reputation for hard work, but the family structure is also important. In this essentially patriarchal society the young are well cared for, with the somewhat paradoxical result that there is little genuine poverty even if unemployment is high. Quite a number of successful local businesses have developed – in cloth or real estate in particular. These often began as small family concerns and the family as a whole shares in their success.

Yet within minutes of Tirano there are communities with a quite different way of life. Just to the west, the road up to Bianzone and San Lorenzo leads to a labyrinth of traditional wooden dwellings with interconnecting balconies – on which the lavatories are usually found – on each floor. At least three generations from one family may inhabit a single house, where, as in many peasant communities, human beings are sandwiched between the hay loft and the stables on the ground floor – a primitive but effective form of central heating when the animals are brought in for the

Sun-dried corn at Stazzona in the Valtellina.

165

The isolated sanctuary of Santa Casa di Loreto soars above Tresivio in the Valtellina.

winter. A young boy once befriended me on a visit here and took great pride in showing off his family's cows, which seemed to be enduring a miserable existence in near darkness. On the same occasion an elderly woman with a pair of Siamese cats as her only visible companions told me how the village was slowly dying.

Equally instructive is Roncaiolo just north of Tirano, set at a height of over 1700 metres on the way to the Pra Campo, a small and beautiful valley reached by a tortuous road through Baruffini. To see the old village – with a population of six and barely a dozen houses – leave your car by the church and continue on foot. The principal street, which forms part of one of the old smugglers' routes, is no more than a metre or so wide and is paved with large, irregular stones. Most of the houses belong to families who once lived here but now visit only at weekends. On one Sunday an 86-year-old woman (she had ceased to live permanently in the village only two years before) allowed me to visit her house. The main room was low and vaulted. On the stove *polenta* was being prepared and sausage and chilled red wine stood on the large central table. There was a single bed in the corner and a beautiful kitchen dresser and cupboard against the wall. The stone ceiling was black with 200 years of smoke.

Just what will happen to such villages is not clear. Some houses have been sold, and as long as care is taken to restore them in the traditional style they will continue to be preserved. One in Roncaiolo has been bought by a doctor from Tirano. But many belong to families whose members cannot agree on what should be done and are being left gradually to decay. Like the kitchen ceiling in Roncaiolo, the public washing place in the centre of the community near Bianzone is a reminder of the past. But its black marble slabs, worn smooth by centuries of scrubbing, are also in a way a symbol of defiance at the possible intrusion of the modern world only a few kilometres away.

Before leaving Tirano, visit the Palazzo Besta in Teglio, a restored sixteenth-century house – by far the finest in this part of Lombardy – which is now a museum and cultural centre. Frescoes in the Salone d'Onore depict twenty-one scenes from the story of Angelica in Ludovico Ariosto's *Orlando Furioso* (1516), those in the courtyard scenes from Virgil's *Aeneid* (left unfinished when the poet died in 19 BC). Intriguingly, the house has a winter and a summer side, with rooms designed accordingly. Those facing north are entirely panelled in wood and have original stone stoves in the corner; those facing south have larger windows, no stoves and far more stone and plasterwork. The kitchen, too, contains a full range of authentic equipment, including a splendid chest divided into four sections for flour of different qualities.

Teglio is a busy village. Its altitude (851 metres) ensures a fresher climate than in the valley and it has its own small skiing area reached by a chair-lift from the village centre. There are some fine beech woods nearby and a path leads to a fourteenth-century tower from which there is a magnificent view over the Adda valley.

Northwards from Tirano the road continues through Grosotto, where there is another superb baroque wooden organ loft, to Grosio. Just before the village is a park dominated by the ruins of a fourteenth-century Visconti castle. Here, too, are some

Dormant orchard at Sernio, one of the main apple-producing areas in the valley of the Adda, just north of Tirano.

of the prehistoric carvings (*incisione rupestri*) of the region – chiefly depictions of primitive figures and fertility symbols – incised in a great slab of rock over which people are surprisingly allowed to roam at will. In the village itself the fifteenth-century Palazzo Visconti-Venosta, now the public library, has been finely restored. The roof is adorned with dragon-shaped, metal gargoyles similar to those on the roof of the Palazzo Besta in Teglio. And tucked away on the south side of the village is the beautiful church of San Giorgio. Dating originally from the eleventh century, the external dimensions give no clue whatsoever to the sense of space inside.

From Grosio, a minor road leads north through Ravoledo to the Val Grosina and a small hydro-electric station and *rifugio* at Fusino, where the valley and the road split. A few hours' walking takes you either to the foot of the steep sides of the Vetta Sperella to the west, or to the Cima de'Piazzi, where serious climbing is possible, to the north. In spring and summer the lower slopes are alive with insects and birds and bright with wild flowers. If you are lucky, you will discover deliciously sweet wild strawberries. The *baíte* in this area are interesting too. Some have been extended using local stone, slate and wood, but since there is no control over building here, in contrast, for example, to the situation in the Stelvio park, concrete, asbestos and corrugated iron also make an appearance. Many are still used for farming, often occupied for two months on end by the women of the family. At weekends they will be assisted by their menfolk and children, with the latter returning home from school or university at particularly busy times. Others are holiday houses, popular not only with people from Como or Milan but also with the Swiss. Unfortunately, some of the restorative work is beginning to leave scars in the form of domestic rubbish or heaps of rubble.

Before leaving Grosio and after a few hours' walking you can do worse than sample some of the best cooking in the area at the local Sassella restaurant, known as 'Sam's'. In particular, try the venison – either as an antipasta (*slinzega di cervo*) or as a main course – the mushrooms and the *pizzocheria*. And encourage the owner to produce one of his good bottles of Inferno to accompany your meal.

Between Grosio and the 'new mountain', the S38 follows the Adda. After 5 kilometres you will see some large pink-and-white buildings on the left. These are the hospital at Sondalo much developed by Mussolini and for which I personally have reason to be eternally grateful. A number of years ago my second son seriously injured himself in a skiing accident at Bormio. Two major operations within seven hours by surgeons here and the transfusion of several litres of blood saved his life. He has gone on to become a highly competent skier!

After Courmayeur, Bormio is now probably Italy's most important ski centre. Well served by hotels and blocks of apartments, it throngs with people during the winter and is never quiet even out of season. The old town, which had a population of around 2000 in 1930, is pedestrianized and tastefully restored, with a series of arcades and pleasant squares to wander through. Frescoed houses date from the fifteenth century. The seventeenth-century church of San Ignazio is notable for the seven large painted wooden figures in a box pew on the north side; opposite, as at Tirano, a carved hand on the pulpit holds a crucifix. Walk round the east end of the church, under an archway with a primitive carving of Christ's face on the far side, and across a narrow and heavily worn cobbled bridge. The narrow road uphill from here leads to the fourteenth-century Santuario del Crocifisso with its impressive frescoes, tucked away in the little suburb of Bormio known as the *contrada Combo*.

Bormio is also the principal gateway to the Stelvio national park, established in April 1935 as a vast nature reserve. The largest park of its kind in Italy, it covers over 100,000 hectares, of which about one quarter forms a great irregular crescent in the north-eastern corner of Lombardy. One-tenth of the park is covered with glaciers, 193 of them in all, including the Ghiacciaio dei Forni, the biggest in Italy and one of the longest in Europe. Recent scientific investigation suggests that on average the glaciers are receding by about 20 metres per year.

To the north of Bormio is the Cresta di Reit, a prominent ridge rising to over 3000 metres, which on a clear day looks like a series of huge, rough-hewn flint tools. A tortuous road winds northwards past a series of hydro-electric stations (the Cantoniera II at over 2000 metres is especially spectacular) and leads to the 2758-metre Stelvio pass, the second highest in Europe. On the way, 4 kilometres from the centre of Bormio, are the thermal baths, where treatment for rheumatism, various skin ailments and gynaecological problems is available. The water, which most agreeably is also used for the town's swimming-pool, is at a constant temper-

---

The Stelvio pass is only open in the summer months; even then there may be snow on the ground.

ature of 38°–44°C. The principal seasons for treatment are December to mid May and June to October, but people also come here to see the original Roman baths, hewn out of the rock. The baths are surrounded by magnificent parkland and, despite modernization, the hotel which opened to wide acclaim in 1930 still retains much of its stylish period charm.

Branching off the Stelvio road before the baths is the S301 to the north-west and Livigno. Because of its remote position, Livigno was made a tax-free zone in 1952. This factor and its situation, which virtually guarantees good snow from November to May, attracts winter-sports enthusiasts each year in tens of thousands. Over 120 kilometres of ski-runs have been established, catering for as many as 13,000 skiers at any one time. In summer the valley and lower slopes provide easy walking. The natural setting is beautiful, but even more magnificent countryside can be seen by leaving the S301 and following the road to Fraele north into the Stelvio national park. The road curls through twenty or so bends up to a pass at just under 2000 metres where it is overlooked by two medieval towers. All around are vast expanses of rhododendrons, pines and heather, with scenery of particular beauty sweeping down to the northern shores of lakes Cancano and Giacomo. By comparison, if you take the S300 south-east of Bormio to Santa Caterina and the valleys of Zebru and Valfurva, you will quite quickly notice a change in the vegetation, with dense woods of red fir and larch. The main road goes directly south to Ponte di Legno over the Passo di Gavia, but at Santa Caterina a secondary road branches east, to Campec and the former Forni hotel. From here a path leads to the *rifugio* Branca at a height of nearly 2500 metres and the Forni glacier, overlooked by a great series of peaks marking the border between Lombardy and Trentino. This whole area of the park is popular with walkers, paths are well marked and excursions lasting up to a week can be arranged in Santa Caterina.

Apart from the magnificent scenery, this area is also important for its flora and fauna. Nearly 2000 different kinds of plants and trees have been recorded. Wild goats, chamois and marmots are common and local people sometimes claim to find traces of lynxes, wolves and even brown bears. Eagles and birds of prey are a regular sight and there are rare species of birds such as the white partridge (*pernice bianca*), or the francolin (*francolini di monte*), whose white winter plumage turns grey-black in summer. Inevitably the motor car and tourist bus make their incursions, but an hour's walking leads to areas of natural beauty unequalled elsewhere in Lombardy. As the snows melt, rivers change from gentle streams to the rushing water courses evoked by the Italian *torrenti*. Colours range from the dazzling white of snowfields, through the pale yellow of lichens and the brilliant reds and oranges of wild flowers, to the browns and fawns of frosted leaves and the dark green of patches of spruce. In the summer, the weather can be gloriously warm.

To rejoin the S38 at Tirano, follow the S300 south. The road winds down from the Stelvio park about 10 kilometres before you arrive in Ponte di Legno, and there joins the S42 for Aprica to the west. On this south side of the park, along the valley of the Oglio, the slopes are in general gentler. There are several easy walks lasting only a day, horses can be hired in Ponte di Legno and it is well worth tackling the 11-kilometre route by a well-worn track up to the *rifugio* Corno d'Aola at a height of 1950 metres. Here the panoramic views in all directions are superb. Ponte di Legno, which lies at the confluence of three rivers, has for long been a centre for excursions and winter sports, but the village itself is not particularly attractive, with clusters of corrugated-iron roofs; nor is the neighbouring low-budget ski resort of Tonale, 10 kilometres away on the very border with Trentino and little more than a series of indifferent restaurants and hotels. There is, however, an ossuary and a grim memorial to the dead of World Wars I and II which rather unfortunately resembles an air-raid shelter.

About 5 kilometres down river from Ponte di Legno is the pretty, busy village of Temu, where a minor road runs east of the river and ventures into the forested slopes of Monte Calvo. Here there is still sufficient wildlife – hares, goats, deer, pheasants, partridge and even, so it is rumoured, some wolves – to attract hunters, not all of whom remember to pay for the privilege. The area south-east of the road between it and the Trentino border is also rich in prehistoric carvings denoting war, fertility and family life, and testifying to a civilization which dates, so it is said, from 6000 BC. Access to this savage and beautiful countryside is possible only on foot.

At Edolo 15 kilometres south of Temu the route leaves the river, which in winter runs high and noisily over its paved bed. The main square of this little town is flanked by pleasant cafés which look out on a fountain and a bronze statue (1903) of a deer being attacked by an eagle. Narrow, unspoiled streets lead over the ancient bridge and up to the church of San Giovanni Battista, richly decorated with frescoes depicting scenes from the saint's life by Girolamo Romanino (1480–1566). Somewhat unexpectedly, a small conservatorium of music has been established in Edolo. Concerts by local people are frequent and the distant strains of instruments being practised can be heard at all times and seasons.

A pleasant and unspoiled village, Edolo could hardly be more different from Aprica, fifteen kilometres along the S39 to the west, where new wealth resulting from the development of winter sports has brought a rapid but often unthinking expansion. What little remains of the old village, described in 1877 as 'poor', is being largely left to decay; investment is concentrated in row upon row of apartment blocks, garish restaurants and superficially chic hotels. By comparison with Bormio or Caspoggio, Aprica is unquestionably ugly, but like them has generated much needed economic development in the region. Occasionally there have been winters when snow conditions have been poor and in 1987 the main road up from the Adda valley collapsed and had to be rebuilt, but with its relatively low prices Aprica's future as a skiing resort is undoubtedly assured.

Rather than taking the S38 from here to Lake Como, follow the minor roads at the foot of the hills to the south of the Adda as far as Morbegno. Three hundred years ago this little town was the most important in the valley, owing its prosperity largely to agriculture and

A road-side sanctuary with its saint or Virgin removed at Ponte di Legno on the way to the Tonale pass.

wrought-iron products. With industrialization, and despite the medallions in the seventeenth-century Palazzo Malacrida celebrating 'il trionfo delle arti et della scienza' ('the triumph of the arts and science'), Morbegno's importance decreased, but it remains an interesting community and a centre for local excursions. Possible walks through the dense woods on the nearby hillsides are numerous, especially along the many streams draining north, though the countryside is not as varied as on the other side of the Adda flood plain, where orchards and vineyards alternate with patches of woodland. From Morbegno, too, there is a road running south-east through Arzo and Albaredo, which crosses the mountains by way of the 1992-metre San Marco pass and eventually joins the S470 for Bergamo in the Brembo valley. This is the only route through the mountains and in winter can be treacherous.

Above **Spring green and a pocket of pasture in the valley of the Oglio.**

Right **The Santuario della Madonna del Piano on the way to the Aprica pass in the southern Valtellina. The empty niches on the façade make it seem lifeless.**

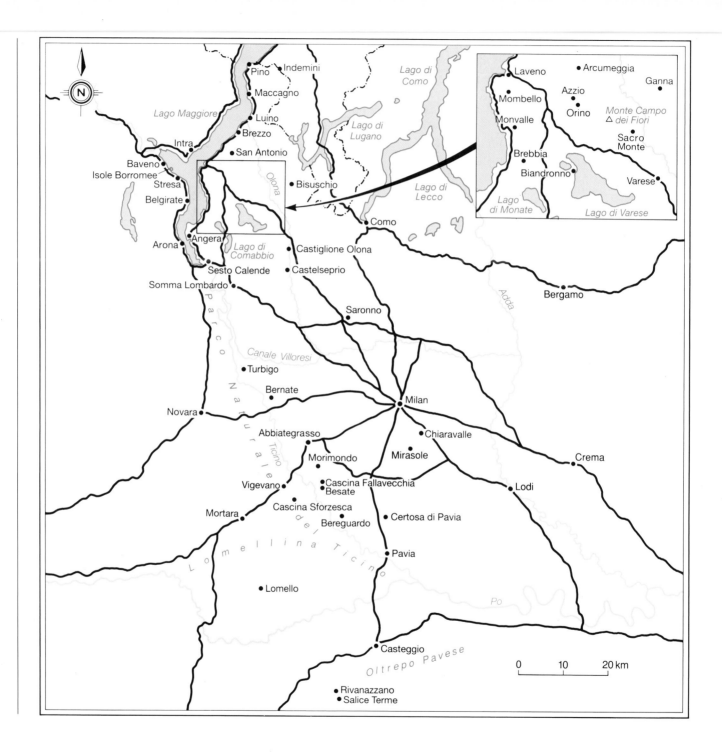

5
Lake Maggiore and the Western Reaches

Castiglione Olona – Varese – Monte Campo dei Fiori –
Sacro Monte – Lake Maggiore – Luino – Maccagno –
Isola Bella – Angera – Parco Naturale del Ticino – Vigevano –
Abbiategrasso – Morimondo – Pavia – Certosa di Pavia

In many respects the two provinces of Varese and Pavia which form the western reaches of Lombardy contain the most varied scenery – mountains on the northern and southern fringes, a vast and fertile flood plain in the centre and a number of lakes, from the imposing Maggiore to the altogether gentler and more intimate Varese, Monate and Comabbio, clustered towards the southern end of their larger neighbour. Access to this whole area is being made easier by the development of a series of motorway links to the north-west of Milan, but the immediate outskirts of the town still remain one of Lombardy's worst in terms of traffic congestion. Heading north on the Autostrada 6, it is advisable to leave the motorway and make initially for Saronno, a thriving industrial town which has grown up around a medieval centre. At its heart is the fifteenth-century church of Madonna dei Miracoli, with a severely classical façade topped by trumpeting angels hiding the older building behind. Inside, sixteenth-century frescoes by Bernardino Luini are amongst the best in the province; those in the chapel to the Virgin, which include the Adoration of the Magi and the Presentation of Jesus in the Temple, are particularly notable, as is the choir of angels by Gaudenzio Ferrari (c.1471–1546) in the dome.

From Saronno, cross over the main S233 and take one of the minor roads running west to the valley of the Olona. Follow the signs north to Castelseprio, where there are the remains of an ancient Longobard camp and the exquisitely simple seventh- and eighth-century church of Santa Maria Foris Portas, with its frescoes of the Virgin and scenes from the gospels. Five kilometres further north the valley deepens and you come to Castiglione Olona, usually described as a tiny Tuscan enclave in a Lombardy setting because of its fine cluster of fifteenth-century buildings: the *palazzo*, church and baptistery inspired by the Tuscan cardinal Branda Castiglioni.

The village is also noted for its frescoes. The cardinal is known to have invited a number of painters to Castiglione from his native Tuscany and the village also attracted itinerant artists, many of whom contributed to the magnificent paintings. The scenes depicted vary. Most of the frescoes illustrate religious subjects, with some of the scenes delightfully set in contemporary renaissance settings. Some of the best are in the church of the Collegiata, which dates from 1421. Particularly good are those illustrating episodes in the lives of St Lawrence and St Stephen by Paolo Schiavo and Lorenzo Vecchietta respectively, but it is the works of the Florentine Masolino da Panicale (1383–1447) that draw many people here. His scenes

Left **Evening sunlight on Lake Maggiore, with the hills of Piemonte to the west.**

Above **A delightfully quiet street in Castiglione Olona.**

from the life of the Virgin Mary in the chancel and from that of St John the Baptist in the baptistery are remarkable not only for the delicacy of the colours but also for the naturalism with which the subjects are depicted, suggesting Panicale was far in advance of his time.

The village has gained, with justification, the reputation of being something of a show-piece, and in addition to the quality of its buildings, statues and frescoes, it keeps various traditions alive. Mock tournaments are held from time to time and the grape harvest in October is marked by a barrel race (*il palio*) through the streets, with the participants in medieval costume.

Standing outside the west door of the church is a very large statue of St Christopher, whose presence you will notice in paintings and chapel dedications in quite a number of churches in this region. Why this should be so I have not been able to discover, but it is tempting to suppose that it is a reminder of the time when journeying north through the mountains or west across the marshy wastes of the Ticino valley which marks the western frontier of Lombardy would have been a hazardous business. The idea that this is 'frontier' country is also supported by the chain of Visconti castles running south-west from Lake Lugano through Varese and south to Vigevano on the banks of the Ticino. It is easy to imagine these standing guard four or five centuries ago against the threat of barbarian raids from the mist-laden and unknown north and west. Most of them are at least partly ruined, but they are generally easily accessible, lying either in or just outside a village. With the aid of a large-scale local map obtainable from any of the tourist offices, this fortified line can easily be followed and makes an unusual and worthwhile excursion.

Today traffic or violent thunderstorms are the only hazards likely to be encountered between Castiglione and Varese, a town built on a series of small hills to the east of the lake which shares its name. It also has another feature. Every so often one comes across a town which exudes wealth or gives off a sense of financial ease which seems to be shared by most of the population. Vichy in France is one; Freiburg in Germany another; Varese is a third. A token of this prosperity is the number of substantial and beautiful villas set in magnificent gardens to the north-east of the town overlooking both the centre and the lake. Many of these were built in the eighteenth century by wealthy merchants from Milan. Most are privately owned, but one which can be visited is the Villa Panza, originally built for the Marchese Menafoglio and now an internationally important gallery of modern art containing works by the American painters Robert Irwin and Dan Flavin and the Swedish painter and sculptor Claes Oldenburg. The first two are both abstract artists who experiment with lighting to enhance the appeal of their work. Irwin is also known for painting on curved surfaces and lighting them in such a way that his works appear to melt into the wall behind them. Oldenburg is generally regarded as the 'Pope of Pop Art', indulging in extravagant, giant canvases and in outrageous exhibits which he offers as a comment on modern industrial society. But nothing in the Villa Panza is of more than modest dimensions.

On the west side of the town is the Villa Litta-Modignani, which houses the town museum and is surrounded by rather unkempt gardens dominated by a giant cedar tree reputed to be several centuries old. From here, looking towards the lake, there is a view of some of Varese's smart modern developments, including an unusual block of apartments shaped like a beehive. Looking towards the town on the other side of the building, you are confronted by a total contrast. Romantic disorder is replaced by the classical rigour of the formal gardens of the Palazzo Estenso, where box hedges, ponds, lawns and gravel paths are laid out with geometrical precision. Built between 1766–72, the palace now houses the municipal offices and public library and its magnificent baroque reception room is used for everything from chamber concerts to the distribution of local health cards. Seen from the garden side, with its pink-and-white façade punctuated by dark green shutters and crowned by a military eagle, the *palazzo* is impressive, and it is not difficult to conjure up a picture of the Varese élite arriving by

This effigy of St
Christopher at Castiglione
Olona is one of many
found in the area
bordering what were once
treacherous lands to the
north-west.

carriage 200 years ago. This is not to say that the town belongs, architecturally at least, to the past. There are several exciting modern residential developments and there is a fine commercial complex on the north side of Piazza XX Settembre. Elsewhere, too, you will find traditional dwellings tastefully – though expensively – restored. Visit, for example, the *cortili* of some of the blocks on the east side of Via Garibaldi just before it joins Piazza XXVI Maggio. Here the traditional external connecting landings have been retained, the roofs re-timbered and re-tiled, and the doorways rebuilt. Some of the ground-floor premises are now doctors' consulting rooms, photographers' studios, or occupied by antique dealers.

Varese has the reputation of being not only one of the wealthiest towns in northern Italy, but also one of the most conservative; indeed, in the 1970s it was recognized as being noticeably right-wing in its political inclinations. An earlier and more violent right-wing period, that of Mussolini's fascist regime, was responsible for much rebuilding and for a series of grandiose edifices. Large statues of classical heroes crowning these buildings symbolized the dictator's prestige and power. Visit, for example, the post office opposite the main railway station, the huge granite clock tower in Piazza Ragazzi dei Novantanove, or the red-brick 'castle' housing the law courts in Piazza Cacciatori delle Alpi. This travesty of a medieval fortress has an imitation dry moat, heavily barred windows on the lower floors and a portcullis protecting the main door. Fortunately, not all the architecture from this period is so pretentious. Some of the rebuilt arcading in the centre of the town could be a century or more older. And, despite modernization, Varese has retained much of its medieval character around the cathedral of San Vittore, one particularly attractive feature being a delicately carved fifteenth-century terracotta window-frame in Via Albuzzi. The cathedral itself, dating from the sixteenth century, is not particularly noteworthy, except for the multitude of painted plaster cherubs adorning its heavily baroque interior – a curiously plain and even ugly host looking down from the roof and the ledges on which they are perched. The ornate high altar is dominated by a figure of Christ emerging from a blazing sun in a curious mix of Christian and pagan symbolism. There is also a fine modern crucifix. San Vittore and its adjoining baroque campanile form the heart of the pedestrian zone where the locals gather to talk or meet for drinks before dinner. As you approach this area from the fringes of the city centre, the noise level rises perceptibly. It is as though the real Varese were turned in upon itself, almost dismissive of anything that does not concern it intimately or directly.

In terms of its buildings, its collections and a simple air of well-being, Varese is an attractive town. Conservative it may be, but it is easy to appreciate why. Like Como, it is much sought after as a conference centre. On the north side of the town, in imposing grounds, is the Villa Ponte, an elaborate, pilastered, sixteenth-century building washed in pale pink and topped by a parapet and pinnacles. This is now owned by the local Chamber of Commerce and is regularly used for national and international occasions. It is also sometimes the setting for open-air concerts. On a spring Sunday morning, with the mist rising from the lake below, it epitomizes the quiet luxury that is so characteristic of much of Varese.

In addition to its inherent appeal, Varese is a convenient point from which to explore the north-west corner of Lombardy running up to the Swiss border. Bisuschio and the renaissance Villa Cicogna Mozzoni with its neat formal garden, decorated, arcaded courtyard and frescoes by the Campi brothers, or Ganna and its eleventh-century Benedictine abbey and small but fascinating collection of objects from prehistory to the nineteenth century, are both within a dozen kilometres on the roads north to Porto Ceresio and Ponte Tresa respectively. To the west is the lake which, like the other small meres in this area, lies in a shallow depression originally caused by glaciation and has none of the dramatic qualities of Maggiore. Its

Early morning sunlight warming the neo-classical façade and piazza of San Vittore, Varese.

SANCTO. VICTORI. MARTYRI. PATRONO

Left In Piazza San Vittore, Varese.

Above Bisuschio, site of the elegant renaissance Villa Cicogna Mozzoni with its formal gardens and belvedere.

shores are generally marshy and approached through gently sloping fields of maize or clover. There is the occasional camp site, particularly on south-facing slopes, but out of season the atmosphere is delightfully quiet. A perimeter road circles the lake and on the western side, near Biandronno, there are signs to Isolino Virginia, a marshy, reedy island which archaeologists believe was formed artificially over the centuries by the accretion of the remains of a series of villages constructed on wooden piles. Certainly there is evidence that man lived here as long ago as 500 BC, and the museum on the island has an instructive and well-displayed collection of primitive tools and domestic objects dating back hundreds of years.

North-west of Varese is the first of a series of thickly wooded ridges running west to east, with Lake Maggiore and Piemonte beyond. The hills all rise to around 1000 metres, one of the highest being the 1226-metre Monte Campo dei Fiori, the centre of a natural park. The ideal time to visit this area is in spring or early summer before the weather becomes too hot and before the coaches of tourists arrive. Monte Campo is also most attractive in winter, when it is frequently snow-covered or when, surrounded by cloud or mist, it seems remote and mysterious. As its name suggests, the mountain is known for its wild flowers and there is a series of beautiful walks along a sharp ridge which bisects the park. The area is protected, and while it does become busy in July and August, it retains a freshness that is a welcome relief from the more humid atmosphere characteristic of the lakes at that time. The paths are clearly marked and there are several vantage points with views on fine days as far as the Alps. Part of the park has been developed for scientific research, and at weekends it is possible to visit the observatory on the top of the mountain and the rather unusual 'cold greenhouse' (*serra fredda*), in which alpine plants are cultivated and studied.

The observatory is accessible by car (though the last 10 kilometres of road are badly in need of resurfacing) and beyond is a track running west to the remains of the Forte di Orino, a medieval tower. Beyond, a path leads down to Orino itself and from there to Azzio, only a short distance from the main road to Laveno and Varese. Walking here can occupy a day quite easily, but do not miss seeing the former Grand Hotel Campo dei Fiori on the ridge and exploring the village of Sacro Monte. The 'hotel', now privately owned, dates from 1908–12, its *art nouveau* architecture with strange chimney designs and elaborate wrought iron particularly striking in such magnificent natural surroundings. Some might say that its very extravagance is out of place. It was built to cater for the increasing tourist trade from which the region had begun to benefit around the turn of the century, though it seems not to have been successful for long.

Sacro Monte can be reached either by car or bus, but for the stronger in spirit (and limb) there is a pathway which starts a few kilometres out of Varese on the road to Brinzio. Linking fourteen chapels along the way, it climbs up a few hundred metres to the sanctuary of the Virgin Mary. Tradition has it that the site of the village has been a sacred place for centuries, ever since St Ambrose placed an altar here and gave the statue of the Black Virgin to the community. Throughout the early Christian period and during the Middle Ages, various hermits lived on the mountain and it gradually assumed a spiritual significance and became one of several sites acting as a barrier to the pagan forces from the north. Even today it appears to hold a special attraction for Christian youth groups. By the seventeenth century the line of chapels was complete, marking the pilgrimage route to the sanctuary. On a hot day it is – fittingly of course – quite a test. And, in an artistic sense at least, some chapels are more rewarding than others. The fifth and seventh are notable for their frescoes, the third for its representation of Christ's nativity and the tenth, on the theme of the Crucifixion, for forty-two terracotta statues by Dionigi Bussola (1645–87).

At the top, crowning the village, is Santa Maria del Monte itself. Although much modified in the sixteenth

---

Place of pilgrimage: the village of Sacro Monte, north of Varese.

and seventeenth centuries, the present church was constructed a hundred years earlier and beneath the high altar are the remains of a building dating from around 1000. There is a magnificent collection of fourteenth-century frescoes here, but what is even more striking is the black marble statue of the Virgin on the high altar, draped in a sumptuous shawl made from crystal. When you enter the church by the west door, and especially if it is bright outside, the figure glows and sparkles with reflected light and appears positively supernatural. As in the cathedral at Varese, the ceiling and walls of the church are adorned with cherubs, though the ones here are better looking.

Just beside the west door is the Museo Baroffio displaying pieces of masonry, collections of porcelain and ecclesiastical robes, and a large number of paintings, many of them unattributed and in a poor state of preservation. The museum is much vaunted, but perhaps an increase in the entrance fee – which has remained at 500 lire for several years – could be used to finance much-needed restoration. A passage between the church and the museum leads to a small square dominated by a huge bronze statue of Pope Pius VI (1775–99). Facing it is the church shop, selling everything from Sacro Monte pepper-pots to crucifixes and rosaries.

The valley to the north-west of Campo dei Fiori is the most attractive route from Varese to the hilly north-western corner of Lombardy. The road to Brinzio and Castello Cabiaglio winds gently up through thick woods and eventually joins the main road to Luino at Cuvio, a village spoiled by an ugly cement and quarry works. Ignore the main road, however, and follow signs to Arcumeggia, reached by a much more tortuous and narrow road cut through the same thick wood. The village is an oddity. In the mid 1950s it was designated as an artists' community and a house was made available where local painters could work in peace. One result is the series of modern frescoes depicting religious, domestic or sporting scenes which decorate the half-dozen or so narrow, interlocking streets in the old village. Each artist's name is preserved for posterity on a brass plate by the side of his work; in that at least he is more fortunate than his medieval forebears, who usually disappeared into anonymity. Another series outside the church depicts the Stations of the Cross. In spite of this activity and the installation of 'antique' street lights, Arcumeggia has lost little of its basic character. At its centre is a tiny bar, a refuge on a cold day and an opportunity to experience the real life of this tiny community.

The road through San Antonio from here twists tortuously down towards Lake Maggiore between Monte Nudo to the west and Monte di Colonna to the east. In winter the snow can be quite thick and there is the occasional sign to a ski-lift. Interestingly, too, the trees on this north-facing slope change as the altitude decreases, from conifers to birches and then to beech and oak woods, giving a layered effect. And as a reminder of just how deeply rural this part of Varese province is, you may well come across a small herd of goats being taken for milking, or find chickens nesting in the wild. Before reaching the main road (S394), turn north to Brezzo di Bedero, an attractive village famous locally for the baroque concerts given in the church of the Colleginta di San Vittore, otherwise known as the Canonica, most of the performances being by visiting chamber groups from Germany and Switzerland.

Beyond Brezzo the road joins the eastern shore of Lake Maggiore, the second largest of Lombardy's lakes, at Germignaga and Luino. Maggiore's name is thought to derive either from its important position on trading routes from central Europe to the Adriatic or from the River Maggia which runs into it just south of Locarno. The boundary between Lombardy and Piedmont runs down the middle of the lake and the northernmost section is in Switzerland and framed by the Alps. John Ruskin, the late nineteenth-century English art critic and essayist, thought it the most beautiful of all the Italian lakes. Luino has an attractive

One of the chapels on the pilgrim route to Sacro Monte just north of Varese. From this point the path becomes progressively steeper.

centre, though the approach road passes a camp site and permanent fairground (mysteriously described by one guidebook, for me at least, as 'beautiful'). A population of about 15,000 is doubled by tourists during the summer months, in particular by visitors from Germany, Holland and Switzerland. As around the other lakes, this influx occurs when the weather is least attractive, high humidity often leading to spectacular thunderstorms. A local tradition, which in fact is substantially supported by experience, claims that the weather will turn cold if it rains on 15 August; if there is no rain it will remain hot into October. Ideally, you should go to Luino in February or March, when the light is at its best and when the tourists have not arrived.

In response to its increasing popularity and prosperity the village is being steadily restored, but, as in several of Italy's lakeside resorts, there is still some way to go: an attractive and busy harbour, a reasonably prosperous lakeside main street and a number of others in the superficially smartened old centre contrast with much that remains dilapidated, if not primitive. In Via Pellegrini, for example, there are shops selling expensive leather goods, porcelain, health foods and homeopathic medicines, an art shop doubling as a gallery and an ice-cream parlour, all within 100 metres of each other. There is also a battered sign indicating a *trattoria* and wine store in an inner courtyard. These have long since disappeared, the buildings which once housed them are almost in ruins, and one window is blocked by an old wooden door bearing the date 1936.

In other respects, though, Luino is very much alive. There are regular and popular Wednesday markets which attract people from the area round about, and religious festivals and saints' days are often marked by particular rituals: St Joseph's in September is celebrated by the baking of a special biscuit, St Francis's in October by roasting chestnuts in the

One of the many small sheltered beaches south of Luino, popular with tourists in summer.

streets. A transport fair in June has recently been introduced, when historic models of trains, cars, carts and even planes are brought to the village, attracting huge crowds. And for such a small community Luino has also made interesting contributions to modern Italian culture. Pierro Chiara, the regional novelist, was born here, as was the poet Vittorio Sereni. More prosaically, in the late 1980s it has also provided Italian television with three of the country's most popular comedians. One local theory for this creative activity is that Luino has had the shifting population of a 'frontier town' since the early years of the twentieth century and that it has always been open to new ideas and influences.

Luino's frontier position, shared with the whole of this north-western corner of Lombardy, has also led over the years to smuggling. As in the Valtellina, activities certainly continued into the 1960s, and though the approach of a tariff-free Europe suggests that duty-free chocolate or cigarettes may be less important than they once were, there is still the thrill of crossing into (or out of) Switzerland by an unpatrolled path. Indeed, if you have the time, walking is the ideal way to explore this area. Paths are well marked, the terrain is not difficult, and there are a number of *rifugi*. By car there is an attractive road running diagonally north-east from Maccagno 5 kilometres north of Luino to Indemini, but the lakeside to the west is much the same as it is further south. Moreover, Lake Maggiore has now been declared polluted, so swimming is not recommended: only Pino just before the Swiss border has so far escaped this blanket condemnation, much to the annoyance of some rival resorts.

South of Luino the lakeside route passes through the sheltered and attractive village of Porto Valtravaglia. Thereafter the shore becomes much steeper and the road plunges into a series of tunnels to reach Laveno, Mombello and the estuary of the Boesio. Laveno is only half the size of Luino, yet seems bigger and busier. And it has the attraction of a chair-lift to the 1062-metre peak of Poggio Santa Elsa, from where a well-worn path leads to the look-out point at Sasso di Ferro. There are splendid views in all directions, but especially

across the lake to Piemonte and north-east to Switzerland; if you are fortunate, the end of the lake may be blanketed in mist, like a land of mystery waiting to be explored.

Laveno also has the advantage of a convenient car ferry to Intra, thereby offering the opportunity to explore the western, Piemonte shore of Lake Maggiore and the islands in the Golfo Borromeo. With hills rising steeply to 2000 metres, this side of the lake is more sheltered than that to the east and enjoys a climate which encourages the growth of exotic trees and plants, seen to best effect in the gardens on Isola Bella and Isola Madre or in those around the Villa Taranto on the outskirts of Verbania. While on this side too, every opportunity should be taken to visit Stresa (a ferry point for the islands) and Arona to the south. Stresa has a justifiable claim to be the most attractive town anywhere on Lake Maggiore and has enjoyed much popularity since the Simplon tunnel to Switzerland was opened in 1906. From the main road and promenade with its shaded gardens along the lakeside, the Lungo Lago, to the foot of the hills, which rise abruptly at the back of the village, is only a few hundred metres. Visit the eighteenth-century church of Sant'Ambrogio, the Villa Ducale and the modern Palazzo dei Congressi, used regularly for international meetings and one of the venues for Stresa's renowned music festival held in August and September. A twenty-minute journey by cable-car from Stresa Lido at the north-west edge of the village takes you to the summit of Mottarone at a height of nearly 1500 metres, or you can drive to the top along an attractive road which winds up the mountain for 20 kilometres. On clear days, there is a panoramic view of the Alps to the west and north from here and even of the mountains overlooking Lake Garda to the east. There are also magnificent views across the lake to the western edge of Lombardy and in particular of San Quirico. This wooded promontory, 20 kilometres south of Laveno, rises rather less grandly to a height of about 400 metres and overlooks the ancient

Isola Bella from Stresa, the most attractive of the villages on the western shore of Lake Maggiore.

and strategically situated port of Angera, originally called Stazzona, the point from which the Romans observed and controlled navigational activities on the lake.

The journey from Stresa to Arona by way of the lakeside road takes only a few minutes, but it is worth exploring the minor road which runs inland through Brovello and Pisano to Ghevio, across the wooded, grassy slopes of the Vergante hills. At Ghevio, the road curls down to the northern edge of Arona past one of the most curious objects in the whole area – a statue of St Charles Borromeo, almost 21 metres high, erected in 1697. It is possible to go inside the bronze statue, the head of which can become distinctly oven-like in hot weather. In Arona itself the local museum has an impressive collection of prehistoric artefacts and remains from the surrounding region.

From Arona a ferry loops back north via Meina, Lesa and Belgirate to Stresa and the Borromean islands, called after the family who have owned them for 400 years and who still control the fishing rights for the whole lake. There are three in all: Isola Bella (the most famous), Isola dei Pescatori or Superiore, and Isola Madre. As its name suggests, Isola dei Pescatori, described in an early twentieth-century travel book as 'squalid', has developed into a fishing village, though I find the restored lakeside arcades and the chic houses clustered around the church rather self-consciously pretty. Isola Madre has a seventeenth-century villa with some fine period furniture and an art collection which the Borromeo family used as a country residence. But as on Isola Bella, it is the gardens which are most noteworthy. These are laid out on a series of steep, south-west facing terraces, ideally situated for lemon and orange trees as well as for more exotic species such as camphor and pepper. Less formally arranged than the terraces on Isola Bella, they are often described as having an English style about them, though, to my mind, the climate rarely encourages such a comparison. What *is* impressive is the silence you find here even at the height of summer.

Old prints of Isola Bella show that the now landscaped island was once a mere rock. The *palazzo* and

Above Isola dei Pescatori, the smallest and perhaps prettiest of the three principal Borromean islands in Lake Maggiore.

Right Dusk on Lake Maggiore with Isola Bella in the distance at the entrance to the Golfo Borromeo. This area swarms with sailing craft in the summer.

Left Fishing off the western shore of Lake Maggiore at Feriolo. The apparently primitive boat contrasts sharply with the modern bathing chute.

Above Two thousand years ago the Romans enjoyed views like this from Angera.

outstanding gardens were designed for the Borromeo family in the mid seventeenth century by Angelo Crivelli, who transformed the unpromising site. Ten terraces leading down to the lake are full of exotic trees and shrubs, a blaze of colour from April through the summer months and a magnificent sight against the blue of the water on a fine day. The *palazzo* itself is richly decorated and furnished, especially the ballroom, the principal bedroom and the ducal chamber, La Sala del Trono, which is rich in gilt and plaster. As in the villa on Isola Madre, there is also a rich collection of paintings, containing works by Giambattista Tiepolo and the Neapolitan artist Luca Giordono. The exterior of the *palazzo* is if anything even more ornate. As you approach it along a gravelled pathway, you are greeted by a profusion of pillars topped and decorated with cherubs and classical figures, imitation grottoes, massive oyster shells and pinnacles bearing wrought-iron vases of flowers. The entrance façade is crowned by a rampant unicorn ridden by a carefree cherub and flanked by two reclining female figures, one with a harp, the other with a flower. This mix of pagan, Christian and classical allusions is quite stunning and is echoed by other statues and fountains scattered across the terraces. The *palazzo* is not to everyone's taste, but the villa and its gardens offer one of the most extravagant examples of baroque art in the region.

The three islands are linked by boat and a ticket for Isola Madre entitles you to visit them all. You can also continue north across the gulf to Pallanza, from where a road leads across the attractive grassy slopes of Monte Rossa just north of the village. And from the Punta Castagnola jutting into Lake Maggiore just to the east there are uninterrupted views down the lake and of locals and tourists testing their sailing prowess in the winds and currents at the entrance to the gulf. Those not sated with gardens can visit the Villa Taranto between here and Intra. The gardens here were originally planted in the 1930s by a Scot, Neil McEacharn, who took full advantage of the site and exceptionally mild winters, high rainfall and hot summers to establish a wide range of rare and exotic plants and trees. Terraces tumbling down towards the lake bear great clumps of gardenias, rhododendrons, magnolias, azaleas and other flowering shrubs and trees which combine to create a mass of colour in the spring. There are also water-gardens fed by waterfalls, greenhouses and a botanical research laboratory.

Twenty minutes on the ferry brings you back into Lombardy at Laveno, from where two main roads lead to Sesto Calende at the southern point of Maggiore. Frustrating as it may be at times – especially if you are unfortunate enough to come across a *deviazione* – it is worth picking a route along minor roads between these main arteries and exploring scattered villages such as Sangiano, Caravate, Monvalle or Brebbia before they are swallowed up by the extensive housing developments that had begun by the late 1980s. The two small lakes of Monate and Comabbio, as yet relatively unspoiled, also provide a change from their more illustrious neighbour. Around them, too, the scenery begins to alter. In contrast to the mountain and lake scenery to the north, you suddenly become aware of vast areas of grassland and cereals.

You are now in the Parco Naturale del Ticino, established in 1974 and protecting over 6000 hectares of the fertile flood plain of the Ticino. Although intensively farmed, it is rich in wildlife and local people will warn you about vipers. It is so flat that it is easy and indeed convenient to explore it by bicycle. If travelling by car, stay as close as possible to the river and work round to the small town of Somma Lombardo, with its Visconti castle. A fortress was certainly begun here by the eleventh century, though the present building is the result of much alteration 400 years later. It rises massively from the centre of this town, noted in particular for its woollen industry, and must have been an important link in the region's western defences centuries ago.

Just below Somma, the river is dammed and water is channelled off in the Villoresi and Pizzola canals.

Autumn peace in the Ticino valley. There is little suggestion here of the abrupt and dramatic change of character in a violent rain- or snowstorm.

Together with the Ticino itself, these form part of the increasingly complex web of waterways and drainage channels running down to Pavia and the Po valley. A number of hydro-electric stations and industrial plants have been built along the river and, in spite of disclaimers, these have inevitably led to a pollution problem. However, many of these sites are hidden by dense woods and there is little sign of them from the road west of Malpensa airport which goes directly south through Turbigo. Pausing only to see the low, elegant Visconti *palazzo* at Bernate with its adjoining church and hexagonal baptistery, you enter the great rice and maize plains for which this part of Lombardy is renowned. Even at the height of the driest summer, surface water can sometimes be glimpsed, a reminder of what this area must have been like before drainage was properly organized. And in winter, when the weather is bleak, raw and inhospitable or the land is covered by snow, you can easily imagine how isolated and self-contained places like Abbiategrasso, Vigevano or Mortara were four or five hundred years ago.

Of these towns, Vigevano is without doubt the most interesting, though Abbiategrasso is also worth a visit to see the fourteenth-century castle and the church of Santa Maria Nuova with its elegant colonnaded entrance, arcades and terracotta statues. Some 6 kilometres south is Morimondo, the site of a Cistercian foundation established in the twelfth century by monks from the mother abbey at Morimond in eastern France, of which virtually nothing now remains. Built of deep rose-coloured brick instead of the hewn stone more usually used for monasteries in France and with a typical Lombardy façade, the abbey church was beautifully restored in the late 1940s. It stands on the south side of the village where the land slopes down gently to the Ticino and, approached through an archway from the north, it at once conveys that atmosphere of peace and humility traditionally associated with Cistercian communities.

The main door of the church opens on to a central aisle flanked by stout brick pillars which blossom into sprays of ribbing at a height of about 10 metres to support the vaulted roof. The furnishings are rich and the sixteenth-century choir stalls beautifully carved. Attached to the church are some of the remains of the original monastery which once covered much of the site of the present village. The chapter house and the refectory, where there are a number of frescoes, have been restored, but the cloisters are still in need of repair. A view of the length of the church can be enjoyed by continuing beyond the village for a few hundred metres along the road to Besate. From here you can also fully appreciate its position.

Vigevano would have been in existence when the monks first came here. Celtic and Roman remains have been discovered in this ancient place and the town's name is recorded in the tenth century as Vicogebuin. In order to reach it today, as then, you have to retrace your steps from Morimondo towards Abbiategrasso for the only crossing over the Ticino for 20 kilometres or so in either direction. As you approach the town from the north-east, you may catch a glimpse of the onion-shaped copper dome of the clock tower on the Visconti castle, but there is little else to distinguish Vigevano from many another important centre in the valleys of the Ticino and Po. It is isolated, like Crema to the east, for example, in a vast expanse of flat, fertile countryside. It is only when you penetrate to the heart of the town that you realize it is special. I have a vague recollection of having read a description of Vigevano as the Versailles of northern Italy. Although this would be an exaggerated analogy, there is little doubt that the complex of castle, cathedral and Piazza Ducale has a magnificence with which, in Lombardy at least, only Piazza Sordello and its surrounding buildings in Mantua can bear comparison.

There appears to have been a castle here since around 1000, the walls of which enclosed the town. Nearly 350 years later Luchino Visconti wanted to impress the nobles of Milan and remind them of his strength, and he developed the site. The result is hugely impressive. Two keeps, stables for over a

Some of the ornate decoration to be seen around Piazza Ducale, Vigevano.

thousand horses and two falconries are all contained within the outer walls. And to allow the occupants to leave the town quickly there is a covered passage 164 metres long with different levels for horses and humans. The inside of the castle and the passage are currently closed for restoration, but it is interesting to try to follow the latter from the outside and to see how the present town has been built around it. The entrance can be found tucked in at the side of an architect's office in Via Rocca Vecchia. This unique passage probably impressed Leonardo da Vinci, who apparently copied the plan of the largest of the castle's stables to incorporate into his design for an ideal city. Rising above the whole site is the castle's main tower, topped by a dome designed in the fifteenth century by the ubiquitous Bramante, from which there is a bird's-eye view of the fortress. From here, too, you can appreciate how the castle relates to the piazza, which is reached by way of a steep stair cut through the south side of the defences; originally there was also a ramp for horses and carriages.

The piazza was built at the very end of the fifteenth century for Lodovico Sforza (the Moor) and is arcaded on three sides, with slender granite pillars supporting thirty-three arches on the longer sides, twelve on the shorter. The carved capitals at the head of each pillar are all different and the walls above are painted. The Sforza arms are displayed over the main entrance to the piazza in the centre of the west side and medallions between each arch depict important personages from Roman history, members of the Sforza family, or scenes illustrating local tales or popular sayings. The fourth side, to the east, is shut off by the slightly curved, baroque façade of the cathedral, which dates from the mid sixteenth century. The whole piazza, which drops 3 metres from west to east, is covered with stones brought from the bed of the Ticino; a Star of David made from dark pebbles in the south-east corner commemorates the contributions made by Jewish merchants and bankers to its construction. The densely tiled roofs of the buildings around the piazza are scattered with more than seventy chimneys, each one of a different design and intended to represent the

Madonna and Child in the Visconti castle, Vigevano.

towers of the towns governed by the Sforza family.

As an architectural piece Piazza Ducale is delightful, but it has many moods. In the summer it bubbles with life as people gather late on a Sunday morning or in the evening for drinks or ice-cream. In winter, when the mist drifts down over the west front of the cathedral, the bleakness of the medieval world is strikingly present. In a storm, when rain spits and hisses from the gutters, it is wild. Inevitably, too, the twentieth century has made its incursions. Fashionable cafés and expensive shops selling clothes, books and furnishings fill the arcades. The piazza is also used for meetings, open-air chess competitions and concerts, none more out of place than those performed by small groups in one of the piano-bars and broadcast to all at large over a loudspeaker system.

By comparison with such secular elegance, the cathedral, unusually in an Italian town, is largely unexceptional, apart from the chapel to St Charles Borromeo on the north side, where some mostly anonymous paintings are crowned by a particularly fine depiction of the Nativity attributed to Macrino d'Alba (1495–1528). On the opposite side of the nave, the chapel dedicated to St James and St Christopher is equally pleasing, its walls and altar decorated with scenes from the Old Testament and the saints' lives. In no way is this a pretentious cathedral, and its intimate atmosphere may at least in part be attributable to the mottled browns, fawns and pinks of the marble used here and in other churches of the region. Of those in Vigevano, do not miss San Cristoforo, where there are two interesting frescoes. The first, which shows the Virgin nursing a baby Jesus already half her size, once more says as much for the representation of children in medieval art as it does for spiritual values. The second, next to it, is presumably of St Stephen, rapt in contemplation in a bottle-shaped cell and oblivious of a leering peasant who is about to drop a large boulder on him from above. Incidentally, the 'true' remains of the patron saint of this church are to be found in the cathedral.

Whatever its architectural merits, Vigevano has had to face certain changes and shifting values during the last thirty years. Once it was the centre of the Italian shoe industry and until the late 1950s hosted a yearly international fair. Here, too, is the only shoe museum in Italy, where one of Mussolini's buttoned boots is on display. Competition from abroad has taken a severe toll of the traditional source of employment, however, and while some recuperation has been achieved by investment in factories making machines for the mass production of shoes, the impact on the town's economy has been very considerable. More and more people commute to Milan to work and there is evidence that tourism is going to have to play a more important role than in the past. One disillusioned young man had no hesitation in telling me that the town was dead. Some older *milanesi* blamed the locals who, they said, are inward-looking, conservative and interested only in their own family's material well-being. They acknowledged that the town has the position and architectural potential to become a serious rival to Novara to the west, even if it will never have the impact of Pavia. But restoration work on the piazza and castle only started in the mid 1980s and then without overmuch enthusiasm. By comparison with what has been done to so many of the *palazzi* in Cremona, for example, Vigevano has a long way to go. As an indication of what *might* be achieved, look at no. 17A in Corso della Repubblica, with its balconies and some fine plasterwork still intact, or the Istituto Arti e Mestieri Roncalli in Via Populo.

Vigevano stands on the northern side of the Lomellina, the triangular plain sandwiched between the Ticino and the Po. Lomello, from which it takes its name, lies almost in the centre. On the way to this little village with its fifth-century baptistery visit the ornate, brick-walled cemetery just to the east of Mortara. In summer you can drive or cycle for hours in a sea of green, past fields of rice or maize or through plantations of poplars on roads which are often raised above their surroundings. The villages are almost always built on islands of higher ground and more than in other parts of Lombardy they give the impression of being very self-contained, almost as though, even in the twentieth century, their inhabitants were cut off by floods for much of the year. The *cascine*, some of them substantial and evidently extremely prosperous, seem positively introverted, often reached by a single track and with their outside walls turned almost defiantly towards any intruder. One of the most remarkable examples is the Cascina Sforzesca just outside Vigevano on the road to Pavia, which has expanded into a tiny village. It was established in the late fifteenth century by Lodovico Sforza, at the time he initiated the building of the piazza in Vigevano, as an early example of an experimental farm. It appears to have been successful. While still fully operational today and crossed by a main road, the community could be remote both in time and place. There are four major *palazzi*, and a host of outbuildings and dependent houses, many of which are beautifully kept and topped by dozens of intricately designed chimneys in the Sforza style to be seen in Vigevano. If you go there

in early summer Via dei Fiori, with its terrace of cottages covered with roses, lives up to its name, and looks curiously English. Whether Via Orefici has anything to do with successful panning for gold in the Ticino 500 years ago, no-one has been able to tell me.

About 5 kilometres after Cascina Sforzesca there is a small road to Molini and Parasacco which loops round close to the Ticino and leads eventually to a pontoon bridge which takes you across the river to Bereguardo. Here you can see yet another stout, imposing Visconti castle, now housing the municipal offices. Just beyond, a few kilometres north on the road to Besate, is the sixteenth-century Cascina Fallavecchia, well worth comparing with the one at Sforzesca. The motorway to the east of the river will take you to Pavia in a matter of minutes from here, but it is far more interesting to go back over the bridge, rejoin the road from Parasacco and approach Pavia from the north-west. On the south side of the Ticino, just before entering the city, there are pleasant walks in an area known as the Bosco Negri, where the ground is gloriously rich in wild flowers in spring.

Central Pavia is easily explored on foot in two or three days. Indeed, driving a car in the town anywhere other than on the main roads cutting across it at strict right-angles obliges you to enter a labyrinthine one-way system. Parking is easy in front of the station on the western edge of the town, just outside the main ring-road. From the station walk across Piazza Minerva and into Corso Cavour. Almost at once a tight network of medieval streets sloping down to the river appears on the right. In contrast to Vigevano, many of the buildings have been restored and though façades have often been completely replastered, patches of the original brickwork and sections of arches have been left exposed.

At the top of the slope and before the streets drop away quite steeply is the twelfth-century church of San Teodoro, where two frescoes dated 1522 and

The edge of the Lomellina reflected in the still waters of the Ticino.

attributed to Lanzani just inside the west door depict Pavia in the late Middle Ages. One is badly damaged and is being restored. In the other, St Siro, the patron saint of Pavia, blesses a view of the town from the south. This shows a covered bridge – then the only place where the Ticino could be crossed – leading into what was the main artery of the medieval town, today's Strada Nuova. Houses crowd in on either side, with the Porta Milano to the north. Everywhere there are towers – more than a hundred it has been said. Even allowing for a degree of imagination or artistic licence, and although many of the towers have been destroyed, Bernardino Lanzani's early sixteenth-century representation of Pavia is strikingly similar to the town as it is today. Unfortunately, the fresco is so badly lit that it is difficult to make out some of the detail, but I was lucky enough to have a ten-minute lecture from a local priest who caught me studying it. San Teodoro is generally rich in wall-paintings and is one of the most interesting churches in Pavia.

Back up the slope leading away from the river stands the cathedral, best approached from the west through a tiny alley, Vicolo Regisole, and across a square which was once the site of the city's Roman garrison. From the outside this is one of Lombardy's less attractive cathedrals. Begun in the late fifteenth century on the site of two romanesque churches that were pulled down to make room for the new building, it was constructed over a period of 500 years. The more recent brickwork, such as that of the west façade, for example, and the walls which have been cleaned, appear to have been constructed from children's toy blocks. Inside, however, the sense of space is overwhelming. The cathedral was built to the design of a Greek cross and the central cupola, added in the nineteenth century, soars majestically upwards. Mostly it is of plain grey stone, but the chapel of Sant' Alessandro Sauli is filled with rich baroque carving. Paintings depict the saint attending to the needs of the hungry and thirsty and on certain feast days a crystal urn containing his remains is placed on the altar. The ornate canopy over the high altar and richly carved choir stalls also provide relief from the otherwise

rather austere interior. Pavia cathedral is notable too for having introduced me to electric votive candles!

To the north is Piazza della Vittoria, where the market once held in the square is now permanently sited underground. Here, too, is the twelfth-century *broletto*, with some exquisite sixteenth-century arcading and a most attractive inner courtyard. The piazza is virtually the centre of the old town and exploration in any direction is rewarding, but it is best to go back south in order to cross the Ticino by the covered bridge with its four graceful arches spanning the river. Originally built in the mid fourteenth century, when it would have been used for trading, the bridge was destroyed in World War II by American bombs. It was reconstructed, though not quite following the same line, in the 1950s; it leads to the suburb of Borgo Ticino, where the twelfth-century church of Santa Maria in Betleme has a striking west façade composed of a series of flattened brick arches. Almost directly opposite are the pillars of a former, rather grand entrance, possibly to a farm, flanked by a bar and an antique shop. Nearby is an enclave of expensive, beautifully maintained apartments, a floodlit concrete bowling-alley and a small garden shop.

Such a mix is interesting, but another reason for coming to this side of the river is to enjoy the panoramic view of the city, dominated by the huge bell-shaped dome of the cathedral. The banks of the Ticino are also better tended here than on the other side, invitingly grassy and generously planted with trees. During the summer months they are much used for picnics. Boats can be hired and in June there are trips as far as Venice which last up to three days. Unofficial rowing expeditions take a lot longer! Before returning over the bridge look out for the bronze life-size statue of a washer-woman beating her linen on a board. At night it is sometimes floodlit and is a vivid

Il Ponte Coperto, the covered bridge leading south over the Ticino from Pavia. Originally built in the mid fourteenth century, it was fully restored after World War II.

reminder of the harsh quality of life here not so very long ago. Luxury apartments on the opposite bank, facing south, provide a vivid contrast, their inhabitants apparently intent on shutting out both sun and view from March onwards.

Back on the town side of the Ticino, there is an attractive walk south along the river past lawns shaded by plane trees. At the far end, cut up into Piazza Berencaria which leads to the pedestrian (and cycle) zone. Just beyond the square, you reach the south side of the romanesque San Michele, without question the most impressive church in Pavia. The outer walls are of pale grey sandstone topped with brick. Three recessed entrances in the west façade are each composed of five delicately carved arches, the stepped columns of which carry capitals depicting fantastic mythological beasts. A kind of horse on the extreme left is shown attacking a man, who in turn is trampling on a human head. Some of these strange beasts are badly weathered, but restoration will rescue them and you find them again on the pillars inside the church. Largely rebuilt after a great earthquake in 1117, San Michele has witnessed a number of coronations of emperors and kings, including that of Charlemagne in 774 and of Barbarossa in 1155. The internal proportions of its three naves are entirely suitable for such dignified occasions. Rich red mosaic covers most of the floor and the crossing is roofed with a magnificent octagonal brick dome with an image of God blessing all below at the very top. Illuminated illustrations of the painted medieval wooden figures on the rood allow visitors to study the workmanship in detail. Frescoes from the fourteenth to sixteenth centuries are plentiful. Two in particular stand out: one in the north transept of the Virgin holding the infant Jesus and a depiction of the Adoration of the Magi in the south transept.

A few hundred metres to the north of the church is the beginning of the university area which occupies most of the north-eastern quarter of the town. The series of interconnected quadrangles and cloisters were once described to me by a Pavia graduate as 'a mixture of Oxbridge and a slum'! The potential attractiveness of the courtyards and staircases is

unfortunately offset by the flaking plastered walls painted in a dull orange and an abundance of notices and graffiti. Quite different in atmosphere and appeal is the Collegio Borromeo in the south-eastern corner of the town, one of two private institutions where competition for places is fierce. (The other is the Collegio Ghislieri north of the town hall.) At Borromeo, imposing double doors lead into an austere white and brown cloister looking on to a gravel courtyard, the overall effect being more reminiscent of a monastery than a student community. Just opposite is a clinic for the elderly; somewhat incongruously the road leading to it, in which there is a hospital, is called Via Massacra!

In all, there are about 20,000 students resident in Pavia and this population makes a significant contribution to the town's economy. Unfortunately, the slabs of pizza consumed by the young at lunchtime also attract pigeons and these birds gather quite aggressively around anyone who shows signs of sitting down or even of stopping. This is particularly so in Piazza Leonardo da Vinci, the main entrance to the university, where three of Pavia's medieval brick towers still stand. Although thought to be quite stable, recent events must have caused local civil engineers to look on these structures anxiously. In July 1988 there was a small fall of masonry from another tower, the Torre Civica, next to the cathedral, which prompted lengthy discussions. On 17 March 1989 the tower collapsed, killing one person and injuring a few more. The cause of the disaster is not known: one theory is that bad weather had eroded the pointing in the brickwork; another that constant vibration from passing traffic had weakened its foundations. Whatever the reason, this event appears from press reports to have provoked a new – and unusual – sense of urgency in a town where many medieval towers still dominate the skyline.

From Piazza Leonardo da Vinci take Via Mentana,

The view of Pavia from the south is dominated by the cathedral and its nineteenth-century cupola.

where the bars in winter are packed with noisy, cheerful students, to rejoin Strada Nuova. To the right is the castle, built by the Visconti family in the fourteenth century and one of the finest fortresses in Lombardy. Designed around a square inner courtyard, three of the original ranges survive, including the imposing entrance front. The building stands in magnificent grounds where, it is said, the Visconti and Sforza families entertained on a huge scale and enjoyed hunting parties. From the outside the castle is grand if somewhat bleak, and its pleasingly balanced proportions are best experienced inside, where long galleries on the first floor, once bitterly cold in winter, evoke the past. Now the civic museum, the castle houses impressive archaeological and sculpture collections and a particularly memorable picture gallery with paintings of religious and secular subjects from the twelfth to the early seventeenth centuries, including works by Bergognone and Correggio. There is also a model of the cathedral made from cypress wood.

The castle is a popular location for wedding photographs and it is not unusual to see three or more groups queuing to take their turn in front of the main gate. It is also much enjoyed by schoolchildren, who delight in feeding the storks which scavenge in the now dry moat.

To the west, the church of San Pietro in Ciel d'Oro stands in a pleasant square next to a military academy. Early stone work and relics suggest that there has been a religious foundation here since the fifth century, but the present church is medieval. It is clearly wealthy and contains much modern sculpture. More traditionally, there are no fewer than eight wall-cases of sacred hearts in the chapel of the Virgin Mary. On the high altar is one of the most celebrated and precious religious objects in the whole of Lombardy, an ornate white marble ark containing the remains of St Augustine which, according to local legend, were brought to Pavia from Cagliari in Sardinia in the eighth century. In the crypt beneath, where slender stone pillars support a series of tightly-packed brick arches, a casket contains the relics of the Roman philosopher Boethius. Adviser to the gothic King Theoderic after

Left **A typical scene in the Po and Ticino valleys.**

Above **Rain-battered grain north of Pavia.**

St Bovo, patron saint of Voghera on the edge of the Oltrepo Pavese, guards the cathedral with St Siro.

the fall of the Empire, he was accused of treason early in the sixth century and put to death. The pedestal on which the casket stands and the surrounding pillars are covered with the names of visitors, most of them Italian.

From the church, you can walk directly south to the centre of Pavia across the ring-road and along Via XX Settembre. This route takes you through Piazza Petrarca, where there is a market most afternoons, and past gardens surrounded by the municipal offices, the theatre and the old art gallery. Between here and the cathedral the medieval world closes in again in a warren of narrow streets and courtyards, for me very reminiscent of the area around the Brera in Milan.

Just half a dozen kilometres east of Pavia, the Ticino runs into the Po. To the south, like a mirror image of the area fringing Lake Maggiore, is a delightful triangle of equally hilly though less wooded countryside, reached by the S35 to Casteggio. Beyond this small town, which boasts some new houses of futuristic design on its outskirts, the land begins to rise. You are now on the edge of the important wine-producing region of the Oltrepo Pavese, with a succession of small, steep hills planted with vineyards and *cantini* advertising a variety of produce, especially white sparkling wines. Everything is neat and tidy and the whole area is crossed by a network of roads which climb steadily towards the south. Villages are compact, the narrow streets providing protection against both sun and wind. Some, like Rivanazzano and Salice Terme, are small spas, generally open from March to November and treating people from all over the world for a variety of respiratory, arthritic and gynaecological problems. Houses and farm buildings are often constructed of a stone patterned with rust, the soft red and brown tones set against wooded hillsides and fields suggesting something of the foothills of the Pyrenees in south-western France. In the spring, when the air is still, the sky is clear and the only sounds are those of distant barking dogs or of the bells on goats and cattle, this countryside can seem very beautiful. At the southernmost point of Lombardy the land rises in places to around 1500 metres; beyond are the peaks of the Apennines which provide such a magnificent backdrop to the coastal resorts in the bay around Genoa. This area may be distinctly less dramatic than parts of central and northern Lombardy, but for me it is in many respects the most attractive of the whole province.

It is easy to go east towards Cremona from here, either by the S10 or the A21, cutting across the northern edge of Emilia-Romagna by way of Piacenza. The S35 to Milan, following the Naviglio di Pavia, has little to recommend it, but between it and the S9 to Lodi to the east are three historic buildings which should not be missed by anyone exploring Lombardy:

the Certosa di Pavia and the abbeys of Chiaravalle and Mirasole.

Of the three, the Certosa, about 7 kilometres north of Pavia and only a kilometre or so from the main road, is the grandest, despite being the work of several different architects. Gian Galeazzo Visconti gave instructions to Bernardo da Venezia for work to begin on the great Carthusian monastery church in 1396 as a mausoleum for his family, but it had to be interrupted on the duke's death just six years later and was not completed until the late sixteenth century, by Cristoforo Lombardo. The marble west façade, begun by Guniforte Solari (*c.*1470) and generally considered to be an outstanding piece of renaissance work, seems to me to be infinitely more attractive than any part of the cathedral in Milan and rivalled only by the west front of the Cappella Colleoni in Bergamo. It is quite lavishly decorated with medallions of historic and mythological figures, statues of the saints and prophets and Adam and Eve, and scenes from both the Old and New Testaments. The façade is divided into five sections separated by richly-carved pillars and crossed by galleries on two levels; the whole is crowned by a small dome supported by eight columns. The doors are flanked by two pairs of white marble columns which project beyond the line of the façade and are decorated with carvings recalling anecdotes concerning the foundation of the Carthusian order and the lives of the saints. The late nineteenth-century English writer J. A. Symonds once referred to it as 'a wilderness of lovely workmanship'.

The interior is in the shape of a Latin cross, with interconnecting chapels flanking the aisles. As a result of stylistic changes while the building was in progress, the church's decoration is bewilderingly rich. The elaborate tombs of the founder and of Lodovico Sforza are notable, but they are overshadowed by the sculptures and frescoes by important artists such as Bergognone, Luini and Annibale Fontana (1540–87) adorning the walls and pillars. Two interconnecting cloisters adjoin the church on the south-east: the smaller, elegant fourteenth-century Chiostro della Fontana with terracotta ornamentation and the Grande

Chiostro ringed by 123 arches. This is where the twenty-three resident monks have their living quarters, each cell consisting of two rooms, one above the other, with a small porch surmounted by a gallery. A workshop and guest rooms are other reminders that this is an active monastery and there is also a museum. I once attended a service here on a violently stormy Maundy Thursday. The church was packed with people, all of them drenched from having to wait outside for the doors to open. Rarely have I experienced such a sense of genuine spiritual community.

From the Certosa take secondary roads towards the south-eastern corner of Milan's outer suburbs and follow signs to the other two abbeys. Like Morimondo, these are Cistercian foundations and date from the thirteenth century. Mirasole, the smaller of the two, still illustrates that monasteries were working communities and not simply institutions for meditation. In fact, it is really a *cascina* with a small church and cloisters attached. Chiaravalle, founded by St Bernard himself, is more extensive. As the oldest Cistercian monastery in the Po valley it is not surprising perhaps that the influence of Burgundy should be seen in the simplicity of its basic plan, a Latin cross with nave and two side aisles. As at Morimondo, however, traditional Lombardy brick has replaced stone. Much was destroyed at the end of the eighteenth century, but restoration has been successful, particularly of the cloisters, chapter house and refectory. Unlike Morimondo, which still enjoys a rural setting, these two abbeys have unfortunately been swallowed by the spread of Milan's suburbs and appear out of place both architecturally and in terms of what they represent. Yet somehow their dignity persists.

Above A carving of St Bernard symbolizing the foundation of the abbey church at Chiaravalle.

Left Chiaravalle: a doctor of the church dressed in cardinal's robes and hat.

Index